500
cupcakes

500

cupcakes

the only cupcake compendium you'll ever need

Fergal Connolly & Judith Fertig

APPLE

A Quintet Book

First published in the UK in 2014 by
Apple Press
74–77 White Lion Street
London, N1 9PF

www.apple-press.com

ISBN: 978-1-84543-589-9
QTT.LCU2

This book was conceived, designed and produced by
Quintet Publishing Limited
4th Floor, Sheridan House
114–116 Western Road
Hove BN3 1DD
United Kingdom

ORIGINAL EDITION:
Project Editor: Jenny Doubt
Associate Project Editor: Rebecca Warren
Editor: Marianne Canty
Art Director: Roland Codd
Photographer: Ian Garlick
Home Economist: Fergal Connolly
Publisher: Judith More
Creative Director: Richard Dewing
Managing Editor: Jane Laing

UPDATED EDITION:
Food Stylist: Lorna Brash
Photographer: Ian Garlick
Art Directors: Michael Charles
Editorial Assistants: Carly Beckerman-Boys, Holly Willsher
Managing Editor: Donna Gregory
Publisher: James Tavendale

10 9 8 7 6 5 4 3 2 1

Printed in China by 1010 Printing International Ltd.

contents

introduction

Whether it's their individual size, their pretty icing or just their ability to bring back fond memories of childhood, cupcakes really do have ultimate treat-appeal. Every generation seems to love them, and even the most curmudgeonly among us will find it hard to fight off a smile when presented with a plateful of cupcakes.

Cupcakes come in many shapes and guises, but the one thing they all have in common is that they're small, individual-sized cakes baked in a muffin tin or cup-shaped moulds, which are often lined with pleated foil or paper baking cups. You can make cupcakes by baking almost any cake batter in a cup-shaped mould. Classic yellow cake or pound cake mixtures are particularly popular, but gingerbread, carrot cakes, fruit cakes, yeasted cakes and brownies can all be transformed into cupcakes. They can be iced, decorated, glazed, dusted or left unadorned – and whichever you choose, they're sure to be delicious.

As well as making traditional baked cupcakes, you can steam some mixtures to make dense, moist desserts, like bread pudding. You can make other cupcakes using the no-bake method, in which you spoon a mixture of melted and dry ingredients into cupcake moulds and chill or leave them to set. These unbaked cupcakes are usually served uniced, or simply dusted with a little icing sugar or unsweetened cocoa powder.

types of cupcakes

Cupcakes go by many different names. Some describe specific types of cakes, while others are more generic, but whatever name they go by, cupcakes can be found worldwide. Even in Southeast Asia you'll find little cupcakes. In the Philippines, mooncakes – rice cakes steamed in banana leaf cups – are a delicious treat.

Many great classic cupcakes can be served iced – chocolate buttercream cupcakes (page 32) are served with a generous smear of rich chocolate icing. Other ones, such as vanilla cupcakes (page 21) are delicious without icing. Madeleines are classic French cupcakes that are also served plain. Baked in a shell-shaped mould, they are traditionally made with a mixture of egg yolks beaten with sugar and lemon zest, then combined with flour, hazelnut butter and whisked egg whites. You will find a modern recipe for madeleines on page 39.

Queen cakes are a traditional British cupcake made with a creamed butter mixture combination not unlike the vanilla cupcake mixture, with currants and lemon zest added. Traditionally, Queen cakes were baked in small, fluted moulds, but today they are usually baked in paper-lined or greased muffin tins.

icing cupcakes

Although some cupcakes are served plain, it is the icing that makes many cupcakes. Whether it's a thick smear of cream cheese icing or an intricately decorated cake topped with fondant decorations, it's the topping that often causes the greatest delight, not just for the sweet, luscious flavour it adds to a simple cake. Once iced, cupcakes are best eaten right away, and if you intend to store or freeze them, don't ice them first. Whether you are a child or adult, beginner or advanced baker, once you get started on the recipes in this book, you'll realise just how fun baking and decorating cupcakes can be!

basic equipment

Most cupcakes are incredibly simple to make, and you'll only need a few pieces of equipment.

scales, measuring jugs, cups & spoons
Accurate weighing scales and/or calibrated measuring cups, as well as proper measuring spoons, are essential for successful baking. If the proportions of ingredients are incorrect, the cupcake may not rise and/or set properly.

mixing bowls and spoons
You will need a medium-sized bowl and wooden spoon for mixing most cupcake batters. Smaller-sized bowls are useful for mixing small quantities. A large metal spoon is useful for folding ingredients into delicate whisked mixtures. Unless otherwise stipulated, use a medium-sized bowl for the recipes in this book.

sieves
You will need a large sieve for sieving dry ingredients such as flour and a small one for dusting icing sugar or cocoa over baked cupcakes.

baking cases
Pleated paper or foil baking cases are available in many sizes, from tiny petit four cups for making mini cupcakes, to giant baking cups for extra-large treats.

muffin tins

Muffin tins are the most user-friendly tins for making standard cupcakes. The standard muffin tin has 6 or 12 cup-shaped indentations. You can line them with paper baking cups, or simply grease them before filling them with batter. The standard muffin cup is approximately 6 cm (2½ in) in diameter. Mini and jumbo muffin tins are a great way to vary shapes and sizes of your cupcakes. Mini muffin tins have 12 or 24 cup-shaped indentations and are 5 cm (2 in) in diameter, whereas jumbo muffin tins have 6 cup-shaped indentations, with each cup measuring 10 cm (4 in) in diameter.

other cupcake moulds

You can bake cupcakes in other moulded tins. Shell-shaped madeleine pans are widely available. You may also find other tins with decorative, ridged cups in a variety of sizes. Individual stainless steel moulds or ceramic cups can also be used to bake cupcakes.

timers

Perfect timing is essential for success, so always use a timer when baking. Accurate digital timers are inexpensive and well worth the investment.

wire racks

Leave most cupcakes in the tin to cool for 5 minutes before transferring them to a wire rack to cool completely. Wire racks come in a variety of shapes and sizes.

other equipment

Electric whisks can save time and are great for combining all-in-one cake mixtures. The whisk should be set on medium speed unless otherwise indicated. A sharp, serrated knife with a pointed end can help slice the tops off cupcakes or make a hollow in which to spoon filling.

basic ingredients

Most cupcake mixtures have four basic ingredients: fat, sugar, eggs and flour. Other ingredients, such as chocolate, nuts and dried fruit, are frequently added.

eggs
Eggs enrich cupcake mixtures and help to bind ingredients together. For the best results, use eggs at room temperature. When whisking egg whites, be sure to use a clean, grease-free bowl. Eggs should always be lightly beaten before adding to the recipe unless otherwise stated.

butter & other fats
Unsalted butter is usually best for cupcake mixtures; it gives a wonderfully rich flavour. For creamed cupcake mixtures, use butter at room temperature; for cut-in mixtures, use cold, firm butter; and for melted mixtures, dice the butter before gently warming it. Margarine, white cooking fats and mild-tasting vegetable oils sometimes replace butter and are a good choice for those with a dairy intolerance or allergy. Butter and cream cheese should always be softened before adding to the recipe unless otherwise stated.

flour & flour alternatives
Most cupcake mixtures call for self-raising flour or plain flour, with the addition of a leavening agent. Wholemeal flour is sometimes used, but it produces cupcakes with a heavier, denser texture. Non-wheat flours, often combined with wheat flour, may also be used. These include polenta, oatmeal, cornflour and rice flour. Ground nuts may be used in place of flour and are particularly good for gluten-free cupcakes.

sugar & other sweeteners

There are many different types of sugar, all of which add their own unique taste and texture to cupcake mixtures. Refined white sugars add sweetness, while brown sugars add flavour and colour as well. The texture of the sugar will also affect the cupcake. Caster sugar is most frequently used for cupcakes, but coarser-textured sugars such as raw sugar, and moist sugars such as brown sugar, are also used. Icing sugar is generally used for dusting cupcakes and making icing. Golden syrup, maple syrup, honey and treacle can also be used in cupcakes, either in place of, or alongside, sugar. They give a distinctive taste and texture, and are a frequent addition to melted cake mixtures.

other ingredients & flavourings

Dried fruits, nuts and seeds are a popular addition to cupcake mixtures. Dried fruits add natural sweetness, so you may be able to use less sugar than in a plain cupcake mixture. Different dried fruits are often interchangeable in recipes.

Fresh fruit such as mashed bananas, apples, pineapples and berries may also be folded into cupcake batters. Frozen fruit may be substituted for the recipes in this book. Thoroughly thaw and drain before adding to the recipe. Chocolate, another popular ingredient, may be used to flavour or bind cake mixtures or to decorate baked cupcakes. For the recipes in this book, you'll need unsweetened cocoa powder, chocolate chips or chunks and different varieties of baking chocolate in your pantry. Vanilla-flavoured pie filling may be substituted for custard. Always assume that herbs used in the recipes are dried, unless fresh is specified. Other ingredients and flavourings include marshmallows, spices, cheese, vanilla, coffee, citrus zest, almond essence, orange flower water and rosewater, and liqueurs.

making cupcakes

There are four main types of cupcake mixtures. The order in which ingredients are added and the way they are combined – for example, beaten or folded in – will affect the final texture of the cupcakes.

preparing the tin
When the recipe calls for the tin to be greased, you may use any fat you choose. Smear a little butter, margarine or olive oil on a paper towel and wipe each cup thoroughly. Low-calorie sprays can also be used for this purpose. Fill any empty cups in the pan with water.

creamed mixtures
For creamed mixtures, you begin by creaming the sugar and fat together to make a light, fluffy mixture before beating in eggs. Self-raising flour (or plain and a leavening agent such as baking powder) is then folded in, along with any other flavouring ingredients.

The mixture should then be poured into baking cups and baked immediately. Moisture and heat cause tiny bubbles of carbon dioxide to be released, producing cupcakes with a light and fluffy texture.

Sometimes baking powder may be replaced with baking soda plus an acidic ingredient, such as vinegar, cider or buttermilk. These substitutes all work effectively to help the cupcake rise while it is baking.

all-in-one mixtures

This technique is literally 'all in one': Put all the ingredients in a bowl and beat them until smooth. Then fold in additional ingredients such as dried fruit and pour the batter into the tin(s) for baking.

whisked mixtures

The classic cupcake mixture is whisked. Begin by whisking eggs and sugar. Then fold in the flour and other dry ingredients. The air bubbles expand in the heat, causing the cupcake to rise and giving it a spongy texture.

general baking tips

When adding batter to a pan, you may either spoon or pour the batter into the cases. Each case should be two-thirds full unless otherwise stated. When baking, the tins should be placed in the centre of the oven. As oven temperatures vary by model, test cupcakes for doneness a few minutes before the end of the baking time. If a skewer inserted into the centre of the cupcake comes out clean, it is done. If your cupcakes are brown on top but not cooked through, try lowering your oven temperature.

storing

Cupcakes made with a high proportion of fat can be stored in an airtight container for several days. Low-fat cupcakes are usually best eaten on the day of making. For the best results, store cakes without icing, and ice on the day of serving. Cupcakes can also be frozen, without icing, in an airtight container for up to 3 months.

decorating cupcakes

Cupcakes are the treats that you can really go to town on when it comes to decoration. A simple spoonful of icing with a cherry on top or a drizzle of melted chocolate is just the start. Supermarkets and speciality cooking shops sell a host of ingredients and equipment to help you – from food colouring and ready-made icings to edible sugared flowers and brightly coloured sweets. Here are a few ideas that will help you transform the simplest cupcakes into a stunning dessert.

getting started
If you're going for simply iced cupcakes – perhaps with a dollop of icing and a big coloured sweet or whole nut on top – leave the cupcake as it is, with its domed top. However, if you want to go for a more intricately decorated cupcake – perhaps with a patterned icing on top, or lots of sweets – slice off the top of the cake to give you a flat surface. Always wait for cupcakes to cool before icing them.

decorating cupcakes before baking
Unbaked cupcakes can be sprinkled with coarse sugar; whole, chopped or slivered nuts or dried fruit; or a piece of fresh fruit such as a slice of apple or peach. Don't top them with anything too heavy or it may sink into the batter during baking.

fondant icing
Perfect for rolling out and draping over cupcakes, this firm icing can also be coloured and made into shapes to decorate cakes. You can make it yourself, but it's much easier to buy ready-to-roll fondant icing and colour it yourself. Simply add a few drops of food colouring and then thoroughly knead the fondant. Repeat until the desired colour is achieved.

coloured sweets & cake decorations
Sweets and coloured sprinkles are easy ways to decorate cupcakes. Alternately, look in speciality cooking shops for sugar flowers, pastel-coloured almonds and other edible decorations. First top the cupcakes with icing or melted chocolate, then allow it to set slightly before pressing on the decorations. If you prefer a cupcake without too much icing, use only a small blob to attach individual sweets or decorations – they'll look just as good but won't be nearly so sweet.

fresh fruit
Summer berries look delightful (and taste delectable) on top of iced cupcakes. They're particularly good on cakes topped with buttercream or cream cheese icing. Or even simpler, just spoon a big dollop of heavy cream on top of each cupcake and top with a few fresh raspberries or strawberries.

simple fillings
The simplest filling is flavoured whipped cream. Try sweetening whipped cream with a little icing sugar and adding a few drops of vanilla or peppermint essence, rosewater or citrus zest. Honey and maple syrup make good flavourings, as do liqueurs such as Cointreau.

mouldable chocolate
Form ruffles, roses, tiny fruits and vegetables, and many other shapes with this sweet, malleable mixture. If you like, tint and flavour the chocolate after adding the golden syrup. To work with this chocolate, generously dust a flat surface, your hands and any utensils with icing sugar. To make mouldable white chocolate: In a medium bowl over a pan of simmering water, melt 450 g (1 lb) white chocolate. Stir in 120 ml golden syrup until the mixture becomes smooth and glossy. Add a little more golden syrup if the chocolate is still grainy. Cover and refrigerate until ready to use. Makes 600 ml (20 fl oz). To make mouldable dark chocolate, prepare the basic recipe, substituting plain chocolate for white and adding 60 ml (2 fl oz) additional light golden syrup.

serving ideas & cupcake gifts

Cupcakes are often associated with children, but offer a plate of cupcakes to grown adults and you're sure to see their faces light up. Whether it's a rack of warm, wholesome little treats or a glittering cake stand piled high with pretty, pastel-coloured confections, cupcakes are always a hit and seem to appeal to every generation.

cakes on the move
Baked in their own wrappers, these lovely cakes aren't just for eating at home. An individual, portion-sized cake is great for eating on the move – whether it's a treat to go in a lunchbox, an energy-boosting snack to take on a long walk or an easy dessert to serve at a picnic.

dashing desserts
There's something wonderfully informal yet utterly appealing about cupcakes that makes them a great alternative to dessert after a special meal. Who's got time to make a dessert after a starter and main course – and who's really got room to fit one in? Why not bring out a plate of sophisticated cupcakes with coffee instead? You're sure to get just as much praise as you would for a dessert that takes hours to make.

celebrating with cupcakes
Big celebration cakes are a thing of the past. What everyone wants now is a towering pile of cupcakes. For birthdays, pile up cupcakes on a plate and stick them with birthday candles and baby indoor sparklers to really get the celebrations going. This alternative to the traditional cake is particularly good for kids' parties, where little children can struggle with a big slice of cake – or for adult parties where everyone is trying to watch their waistline!

Huge, tiered wedding cakes are off the agenda for those in the know. For a real impact at your wedding, go for pretty white wedding cupcakes piled high on a cake stand or arranged in tiers. It makes serving so much easier – and guests will love them.

special gifts

Cupcakes make great gifts, and you're sure to put a smile on the face of the recipient. They're usually best packed in a single layer, with a little tissue paper tucked around them to make sure they don't shift as you transport them. Pretty boxes with clear plastic lids are a good choice, particularly for cupcakes with decorative icing. They're available from stationery shops and department stores, so look around and see what you can find. Flat baskets make another pretty way to deliver your cupcakes. Arrive at a brunch party with a basket full of cupcakes and your host – and the other guests – will love you for them!

Cupcakes with a firm icing (such as fondant or royal icing) can look pretty wrapped up individually in clear cellophane. Cut out a large square of cellophane, place a cupcake in the centre, then pull up the edges around the cake and tie with ribbon. These individually wrapped cakes make great going-home presents after a kids' party or festive wedding favours.

You can also decorate the foil or paper baking cups that contain the cupcakes. Try tying ribbon around each baking cup, or cut out a round of pretty fabric, place the cupcake in the centre and tie up firmly with coordinating ribbon.

classic cupcakes

These cupcakes have delighted generations.
From the classic combination of apple and
cinnamon to the irresistibly rich pairing of rum
and raisin, all the best-loved recipes are here.

spanish orange syrup cupcakes

see variations page 42

Make these sticky cupcakes in advance to let the syrup soak through.

for the cupcakes
2 medium seedless sweet oranges,
    peeled and roughly chopped
115 g (4 oz) unsalted butter
225 g (8 oz) caster sugar
2 eggs
60 g (2½ oz) semolina

60 g (2 oz) ground almonds
60 g (2½ oz) self-raising flour

for the syrup
1 peeled orange rind, from cupcake recipe
100 g (3½ oz) caster sugar
240 ml (8 fl oz) water

Preheat the oven to 160°C (325°F / Gas mark 3). Place 12 paper baking cases in a muffin tin. In a saucepan, cover the oranges with water. Simmer until tender, about 15 minutes. Cool. Drain the oranges and purée in a food processor. In a bowl, beat the butter and sugar with an electric whisk until light. Slowly beat in the eggs. Stir in the rest of the ingredients, along with the orange purée, until well combined. Spoon the mixture into the cases. Bake for 22 to 25 minutes or until a skewer inserted in the centre comes out clean. Remove tin from the oven and cool.

To make the syrup, thinly slice the orange rind, removing the pith. Cut the orange rind into thin strips. In a pan, bring the sugar and water to a simmer, stirring to dissolve the sugar. Add the orange strips and boil uncovered for 5 minutes, or until tender. With a toothpick, prick 5 holes in each cupcake and pour the warm syrup over them. Then remove the cupcakes and cool on a rack. Store in an airtight container for up to 2 days.

Makes 1 dozen

vanilla cupcakes

see variations page 43

The grand dame of cupcakes. If you can get vanilla sugar, use half caster and half vanilla caster. This will really enhance the vanilla flavour.

225g (8 oz) unsalted butter, softened
225 g (8 oz) caster sugar
225 g (8 oz) self-raising flour

1 tsp baking powder
4 eggs
1 tsp vanilla essence

Preheat the oven to 175°C (350°F / Gas mark 4). Place 18 paper baking cases in muffin tins.

Place all the ingredients in a medium bowl and beat with an electric whisk until smooth and pale, about 2 to 3 minutes.

Spoon the mixture into the cases. Bake for 20 minutes or until a skewer inserted in the centre comes out clean.

Remove the tins from the oven and cool for 5 minutes. Then remove the cupcakes and cool on a rack.

Store in an airtight container for up to 3 days, or freeze for up to 3 months.

Makes 1¹/₂ dozen

gingerbread pots

see variations page 44

You could make these dense, sticky gingerbread cupcakes in terra cotta pots to give them a rustic charm. The sharp lemon drizzle helps to cut the sweetness of the gingerbread.

for the gingerbread
150 g (5 oz) self-raising flour
150 g (5 oz) wholemeal self-raising flour
1 tbsp baking powder
4 tsp ground ginger
1 tsp cinnamon
225 g (8 oz) light brown sugar
2 eggs

115 ml (4 fl oz) honey
115 g (4 oz) unsalted butter, melted
175 ml (6 fl oz) milk
2 tbsp roughly chopped crystallised ginger

for the drizzle
125 g (4½ oz) icing sugar
5 tbsp lemon juice

Preheat the oven to 175°C (350°F / Gas mark 4). Place 12 paper baking cases in a muffin tin or line 12 small terra cotta pots with greaseproof paper. Sieve the flours, baking powder, ginger and cinnamon into a large bowl. In a medium bowl combine the remaining ingredients and beat with an electric whisk until smooth, about 2 to 3 minutes. Stir into the dry ingredients. Spoon the batter into the cases.

Bake for 20 minutes or until a skewer inserted in the centre comes out clean. Remove tin or pots from the oven and cool for 10 minutes. Then remove cupcakes and cool on a rack. To make the drizzle, sieve the icing sugar into a bowl and slowly add the lemon juice, stirring until just combined. Drizzle over the tops of the cupcakes. Store in an airtight container for up to 3 days.

Makes 1 dozen

lemon butterfly cupcakes

see variations page 45

You'll love these delicate little numbers, which can be served with tea or as a dessert.

for the cupcakes
225 g (8 oz) unsalted butter, softened
225 g (8 oz) caster sugar
225 g (8 oz) self-raising flour
1 tsp baking powder
1 tsp salt
4 eggs
1 tsp vanilla essence

for the icing
115 g (4 oz) unsalted butter
225 g (8 oz) icing sugar, sieved
1 tsp vanilla essence
1 tbsp lemon zest

Preheat the oven to 175°C (350°F / Gas mark 4). Place 18 paper baking cases in muffin tins. Combine all ingredients for the cupcakes in a large bowl and beat with an electric whisk until smooth and pale, about 2 to 3 minutes. Spoon the batter into the cases.

Bake for 20 minutes. Remove tins from the oven and cool for 5 minutes. Then remove the cupcakes and cool on a rack. Prepare the icing by beating the butter, icing sugar, vanilla and lemon zest until smooth. Cut a slice from the top of each cake and cut it into two. Pipe the icing onto the flattened top of each cupcake. Then place the half-circles of cake at an angle on each side of the icing.

Store without icing in an airtight container for up to 3 days, or freeze for up to 3 months.

Makes 1¹/₂ dozen

rum & raisin cupcakes

see variations page 46

Use dark rum in this recipe to give these cupcakes a warm Caribbean feel.

for the cupcakes
75 g (3 oz) raisins
3 tbsp dark rum
225 g (8 oz) unsalted butter, softened
225 g (8 oz) caster sugar
225 g (8 oz) self-raising flour

1 tsp baking powder
4 eggs

for the syrup
5 tbsp dark rum
2 tbsp light brown sugar

Soak the raisins in the rum for 2 to 3 hours or overnight to soften them. Drain. Preheat the oven to 175°C (350°F / Gas mark 4). Place 18 paper baking cases in muffin pans. Combine all the cupcake ingredients in a large bowl and beat with an electric whisk until smooth and pale, about 2 to 3 minutes. Stir in the raisins. Spoon the batter into the cases. Bake for 20 minutes.

While the cupcakes are in the oven, combine the syrup ingredients in a pan. Over low heat, dissolve the sugar in the rum. Simmer for 5 minutes, then remove from the heat. Remove pans from the oven. With a toothpick, prick 5 holes in each cupcake and pour the warm syrup over them. Then remove the cupcakes and cool on a rack.

Store in an airtight container for up to 3 days, or freeze for up to 3 months.

Makes 1 1/2 dozen

mini raspberry & coconut cupcakes

see variations page 47

The inspiration for these cupcakes came from the classic English Bakewell tart.

3 tbsp ground almonds
40 g (1½ oz) desiccated coconut
175 g (6 oz) icing sugar, sieved
200 g (7 oz) plain flour
1 tsp baking powder

115 g (4 oz) unsalted butter, melted
5 egg whites
115 g (4 oz) fresh or thawed, frozen raspberries
2 tbsp desiccated coconut, to finish

Preheat the oven to 190°C (375°F / Gas mark 5). Place 24 mini ceramic baking cases on a baking tray.

In a large bowl, combine the ground almonds, coconut, icing sugar, flour and baking powder. Stir in the butter, followed by the egg whites.

Spoon the mixture into the cases. Drop a raspberry and some of the desiccated coconut on top of each cupcake. Bake for 12 to 15 minutes or until lightly browned. Remove the cases from the oven and cool for 5 minutes. Then remove the cupcakes and cool on a rack.

Store in an airtight container for up to 2 days, or freeze in a sealed container for up to 3 months.

Makes 2 dozen

carrot & walnut cupcakes

see variations page 48

Carrot cake somehow doesn't seem to be as naughty as other cakes!

for the cupcakes
225 g (8 oz) unsalted butter, softened
225 g (8 oz) caster sugar
225 g (8 oz) self-raising flour
4 eggs
1 tsp mixed spice
100 g (3½ oz) chopped walnuts
150 g (5 oz) freshly grated carrots
2 tbsp sultanas

for the icing
200 g (7 oz) cream cheese, softened
175 g (6 oz) icing sugar, sieved
1 tbsp lemon juice
1 tsp vanilla essence
3 tbsp chopped walnuts

Preheat the oven to 175°C (350°F / Gas mark 4). Place 18 baking cases in muffin tins. Combine the butter, sugar, flour and eggs in a large bowl and beat with an electric whisk until smooth, about 2 to 3 minutes. Stir in the rest of the ingredients. Spoon the batter into the cases. Bake for 20 minutes. Remove tins from the oven and cool for 5 minutes. Then remove the cupcakes and cool on a rack. To make the icing, slowly beat the cream cheese and icing sugar in a large bowl with an electric whisk until creamy and soft. Add the lemon juice and vanilla and beat briskly until well combined. Spread the icing liberally onto the cooled cupcakes and garnish with the chopped walnuts.

Store without icing for up to 3 days in an airtight container, or freeze for up to 3 months.

Makes 1½ dozen

very cherry cupcakes

see variations page 49

Maraschino cherries give these cupcakes a wonderful rich flavour.

for the cupcakes
225 g (8 oz) unsalted butter, softened
225 g (8 oz) caster sugar
225 g (8 oz) self-raising flour
1 tsp baking powder
4 eggs
2 tbsp kirsch

for the icing
375 g (13 oz) icing sugar, sieved
225 g (8 oz) unsalted butter
pinch of salt
red food colouring
18 bottled morello or maraschino cherries,
    with stems

Preheat the oven to 350°F (175°C). Place 18 paper baking cases in muffin tins.

Combine all the cupcake ingredients in a large bowl and beat with an electric whisk until smooth, about 2 to 3 minutes. Spoon the batter into the cases. Bake for 20 to 22 minutes. Remove tins from the oven and cool for 5 minutes. Then remove the cupcakes and cool on a rack. To make the icing, beat the icing sugar, butter and salt in a medium bowl with an electric whisk until smooth. Add a few drops of the food colouring and beat until well combined and pink. Spread the icing onto the cooled cupcakes and garnish with a cherry.

Store without icing in an airtight container for up to 3 days, or freeze for up to 3 months.

Makes 1½ dozen

classic chocolate buttercream cupcakes

see variations page 50

The plain chocolate in this recipe gives the icing a wonderful glossy sheen.

for the cupcakes
225 g (8 oz) unsalted butter, softened
225 g (8 oz) caster sugar
225 g (8 oz) self-raising flour
1 tsp baking powder
4 tbsp Dutch-process cocoa powder
4 eggs
115 ml (4 fl oz) buttermilk
1 tsp vanilla essence

for the icing
100 g (3½ oz) plain chocolate, chopped
2 tbsp double cream
50 g (2 oz) unsalted butter, softened
100 g (3½ oz) icing sugar, sieved

Preheat the oven to 175°C (350°F / Gas mark 4). Place 18 paper baking cases in muffin tins. Combine all the cupcake ingredients in a large bowl and beat with an electric whisk until smooth, about 2 to 3 minutes. Spoon the batter into the cases. Bake for 20 to 22 minutes or until a skewer inserted in the centre comes out clean. Remove tins from the oven and cool for 5 minutes. Then remove the cupcakes and cool on a rack. For the icing, put the chocolate, cream and butter in a pan over low heat. Stir gently until combined. Remove from the heat and stir in the icing sugar until the mixture is smooth. Swirl onto the cupcakes.

Store without icing in an airtight container for up to 2 days.

Makes 1½ dozen

apple sauce &
cinnamon cupcakes

see variations page 51

Cinnamon brings a delicate sweetness to this cupcake recipe and complements the apple sauce marvellously.

115 g (4 oz) unsalted butter, softened
115 g (4 oz) caster sugar
115 g (4 oz) self-raising flour
2 eggs
115 g (4 oz) unsweetened apple sauce

³/₄ tsp cinnamon
50 g (2 oz) pecans, chopped
75 g (3 oz) sultanas
1 small red eating apple, thinly sliced
2 tbsp caster sugar

Preheat the oven to 175°C (350°F / Gas mark 4). Grease a 12-cup muffin tin. Place the butter, sugar, flour and eggs in a bowl and beat with an electric whisk until smooth and pale, about 2 to 3 minutes. Stir in the apple sauce, cinnamon, pecans and sultanas.

Spoon the batter into the cases. Lay the apple slices on top and sprinkle with a little sugar.

Bake for 25 to 27 minutes. Remove tin from the oven and cool for 5 minutes. Then remove the cupcakes and cool on a rack. Serve warm.

Store in an airtight container for up to 3 days, or freeze for up to 3 months.

Makes 1 dozen

peanut butter cupcakes

see variations page 52

The texture of crunchy peanut butter in this recipe is excellent, though creamier varieties also work.

for the cupcakes
225 g (8 oz) unsalted butter, softened
225 g (8 oz) caster sugar
225 g (8 oz) self-raising flour
2 tsp. baking powder
4 eggs
115 g (4 oz) crunchy peanut butter

for the icing
60 g (2¹/₂ oz) crunchy peanut butter
50 g (2 oz) unsalted butter, softened
2 tsp vanilla essence
115 g (4 oz) icing sugar, sieved
2 tbsp milk

Preheat the oven to 175°C (350°F / Gas mark 4). Place 18 paper baking cases in muffin tins. Combine the butter, sugar, flour and eggs in a large bowl and beat with an electric whisk until smooth, about 2 to 3 minutes. Stir in the peanut butter until well combined. Spoon the batter into the cases. Bake for 20 to 22 minutes. Remove tins from the oven and cool for 5 minutes. Then remove the cupcakes and cool on a rack.

To make the icing, combine the peanut butter, butter and vanilla in a medium bowl. Using an electric whisk, beat until light and fluffy, about 1 to 2 minutes. Add the icing sugar along with the milk, and beat until well combined. Swirl the icing onto the cooled cupcakes. Store without icing in an airtight container for up to 3 days, or freeze for up to 3 months.

Makes 1¹/₂ dozen

poppy seed cupcakes with lemon drizzle

see variations page 53

The poppy seeds give these cupcakes a wonderful crunch!

for the cupcakes
225 g (8 oz) unsalted butter, softened
225 g (8 oz) caster sugar
225 g (8 oz) self-raising flour
4 eggs
1 tsp vanilla essence
1 tbsp poppy seeds
1 tbsp grated lemon zest

for the drizzle
125 g (4^1/$_2$ oz) icing sugar
4 tbsp lemon juice
2 tbsp poppy seeds

Preheat the oven to 175°C (350°F / Gas mark 4). Place 18 paper baking cases in muffin tins. Combine the butter, sugar, flour and eggs in a large bowl and beat with an electric whisk until smooth, about 2 to 3 minutes. Stir in the vanilla, poppy seeds and lemon zest until well combined. Spoon the batter into the cases. Bake for 20 to 22 minutes. Remove tins from the oven and cool for 5 minutes. Then remove the cupcakes and cool on a rack. To make the drizzle, sieve the icing sugar into a bowl and stir in the lemon juice until it resembles the consistency of double cream. Stir in the poppy seeds and drizzle over the cupcakes.

Store in an airtight container for up to 2 days, or freeze for up to 3 months.

Makes 1^1/$_2$ dozen

madeleines

see variations page 54

These light, shell-shaped cupcakes hail from the town of Commercy in the Lorraine region of France.

for the madeleines
4 eggs
175 g (6 oz) caster sugar
125 g (4½ oz) plain flour
1 tsp baking powder
115 g (4 oz) unsalted butter, melted and cooled
1 tbsp grated lemon zest

for the glaze
375 g (13 oz) icing sugar, sieved
225 g (8 oz) unsalted butter, softened
pinch of salt
1 tbsp grated orange zest
icing sugar, for dusting

Preheat the oven to 175°C (350°F / Gas mark 4). Grease a tin for 18 small madeleines. In a medium bowl, beat the eggs and sugar until pale and thick. Sieve the flour and baking powder into a separate medium bowl. Slowly add the flour to the egg mixture. Stir in the lemon zest, and pour in the melted butter. Refrigerate for 20 minutes. Spoon the batter into the tin, filling each mould about two-thirds full. Bake for 20 minutes. Remove tin from the oven and cool for 10 minutes. Then remove the madeleines and cool on a rack. To make the glaze, beat the icing sugar, butter, salt and orange zest together in a bowl using an electric whisk until smooth and creamy. Smear a little glaze on each madeleine and dust with icing sugar.

Store in an airtight container up to 2 days, or freeze for up to 3 months

Makes 1½ dozen

banana cupcakes

see variations page 55

The subtle flavour of banana perfectly complements the cream cheese icing.

for the cupcakes
225 g (8 oz) unsalted butter, softened
225 g (8 oz) caster sugar
225 g (8 oz) self-raising flour
4 eggs
1/4 tsp nutmeg
225 g (8 oz) mashed ripe bananas

for the icing
200 g (7 oz) cream cheese
175 g (6 oz) icing sugar, sieved
1 tbsp lemon juice
1 tsp vanilla essence
1 banana, thinly sliced

Preheat the oven to 175°C (350°F / Gas mark 4). Place 18 paper baking cases in muffin tins. Combine the butter, sugar, flour, eggs and nutmeg in a large bowl and beat with an electric whisk until smooth, about 2 to 3 minutes. Stir in the mashed bananas until well combined. Spoon the batter into the cases. Bake for 20 to 22 minutes. Remove tins from the oven and cool for 5 minutes. Then remove the cupcakes and cool on a rack.

To make the icing, slowly beat the cream cheese in a large bowl with an electric whisk until it is soft and smooth. Add the icing sugar, lemon juice and vanilla. Beat briskly until smooth and well combined. Swirl the icing onto the cooled cupcakes. Decorate each cupcake with a banana slice. Store without icing in an airtight container for up to 3 days, or freeze for up to 3 months.

Makes 1 1/2 dozen

variations

spanish orange syrup cupcakes

see base recipe page 19

blood orange syrup cupcakes
Prepare the basic cupcake recipe, substituting blood oranges for the sweet oranges.

orange & lemon syrup cupcakes
Prepare the basic cupcake recipe, adding 2 tablespoons lemon juice to the orange purée. For the syrup, zest 1 medium lemon and add with the orange zest to the water and sugar syrup.

grapefruit & orange syrup cupcakes
Prepare the basic cupcake recipe. Add 2 tablespoons grapefruit juice to the orange purée. For the syrup, zest half a medium grapefruit and add it with the orange zest to the water and sugar syrup.

lime syrup cupcakes
Prepare the basic cupcake recipe, substituting 6 small limes for the sweet oranges, and use lime rind to make the syrup.

mandarin orange & almond syrup cupcakes
Prepare the basic cupcake recipe, substituting 115 g (4 oz) puréed mandarin oranges for the oranges in the cupcakes and prepared almond syrup for the orange syrup.

variations

vanilla cupcakes

see base recipe page 21

saffron cupcakes
Prepare the basic cupcake recipe. Add a pinch of saffron to 2 tablespoons boiling water. Infuse for 5 minutes. After creaming the cupcake ingredients, stir in saffron and water.

almond cupcakes
Prepare the basic cupcake recipe, adding 3 tablespoons ground almonds to the mixture and substituting 1 teaspoon almond essence for the vanilla essence.

vanilla & sultana cupcakes
Prepare the basic cupcake recipe. After creaming the cupcake ingredients, stir in 75 g (3 oz) sultanas.

vanilla, butter & nut cupcakes
Prepare the basic cupcake recipe, substituting vanilla, butter and nut essence for vanilla.

coffee-time cupcakes
Prepare the basic cupcake recipe, substituting coffee essence for vanilla.

variations

gingerbread pots

see base recipe page 22

fruity pots
Fold 75 g (3 oz) mixed chopped dried apricots, raisins and sultanas into the egg mixture before stirring into the dry ingredients.

rhubarb–ginger pots
Add 75 g (3 oz) cooked sweetened rhubarb to the egg mixture before stirring in the dry ingredients.

banana–ginger pots
Add 1 mashed banana to the egg mixture before stirring in the dry ingredients.

apple–ginger pots
Add 1 grated Golden Delicious apple to the egg mixture before stirring in the dry ingredients.

gingerbread pots with ginger–honey drizzle
Prepare the basic cupcake recipe, substituting 115 ml (4 fl oz) honey and 1 tablespoon freshly grated ginger for the drizzle. Simmer the honey and ginger together in a saucepan for 5 minutes, let cool, then drizzle over the cupcakes.

lemon butterfly cupcakes

see base recipe page 24

orange & lemon butterfly cupcakes
Prepare the basic cupcake recipe. Add 1$^1/_2$ tablespoons grated orange zest to the icing mixture.

redcurrant butterfly cupcakes
Prepare the basic cupcake recipe. Lightly crush 40 g (1$^1/_2$ oz) fresh or thawed frozen redcurrants with a fork and add to the icing mixture.

hazelnut & sultana butterfly cupcakes
Prepare the basic cupcake recipe. Stir 3 tablespoons roughly chopped toasted hazelnuts and 2 tablespoons sultanas into the creamed icing mixture.

blueberry & lemon butterfly cupcakes
Prepare the basic cupcake recipe, adding 60 g (2 oz) dried blueberries.

variations

rum & raisin cupcakes

see base recipe page 26

orange liqueur & crystallised peel cupcakes
Prepare the basic cupcake recipe, substituting orange liqueur for the rum and 75 g (3 oz) chopped crystallised peel for the raisins.

vodka, chilli & chocolate chip cupcakes
Prepare the basic cupcake recipe. Substitute vodka for the rum. Add 1 tablespoon seeded and finely chopped chillies and 75 g (3 oz) plain chocolate chips in place of the raisins.

malibu & pineapple cupcakes
Prepare the basic cupcake recipe, substituting Malibu for the rum and 75 g (3 oz) finely chopped dried pineapple for the raisins.

golden sherry cupcakes
Prepare the basic cupcake recipe, substituting sherry for the rum and 75 g (3 oz) sultanas for the raisins.

mini raspberry & coconut cupcakes

see base recipe page 29

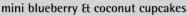

mini blueberry & coconut cupcakes
Prepare the basic cupcake recipe, substituting blueberries for the raspberries
and adding 1 tablespoon finely grated lime zest.

mini blackberry & coconut cupcakes
Prepare the basic cupcake recipe, substituting 50 g (2 oz) blackberries for
the raspberries.

mini lime, mango & coconut cupcakes
Prepare the basic cupcake recipe, substituting 50 g (2 oz) finely chopped
fresh or frozen mango and 1 tablespoon finely grated lime zest for
the raspberries.

mini pistachio & apricot cupcakes
Prepare the basic cupcake recipe, substituting ground pistachios for the
ground almonds and chopped, tinned apricots for the raspberries.

variations

carrot & walnut cupcakes

see base recipe page 30

coffee & walnut-iced carrot cupcakes

Prepare the basic cupcake recipe. Add 1 teaspoon hot coffee, 1 teaspoon instant coffee granules and 1 teaspoon coffee liqueur to the icing mixture. Swirl the coffee icing on top of the cupcakes, and garnish with chopped walnuts.

orange cream cheese-iced carrot cupcakes

Prepare the basic cupcake recipe. To make the icing, substitute 1 tablespoon orange juice for the lemon juice. Swirl the icing and garnish with chopped walnuts and finely grated lemon zest.

mascarpone-iced carrot cupcakes

Prepare the basic cupcake recipe. To make the icing, substitute 225 g (8 oz) mascarpone for the cream cheese.

courgette, yellow squash & carrot cupcakes

Prepare the basic cupcake recipe, using 50 g (2 oz) each of grated carrots, grated courgette and grated yellow squash in place of carrots.

variations

very cherry cupcakes

see base recipe page 31

chocolate chip & cherry-iced cupcakes
Prepare the basic cupcake recipe. Stir 100 g (3½ oz) plain chocolate chips
into the icing mixture after adding the food colouring.

almond & cherry-iced cupcakes
Prepare the basic cupcake recipe, adding 3 tablespoons ground almonds to
the batter mixture. Sprinkle 2 tablespoons of toasted almonds on top of the
iced cupcakes, and garnish each with a cherry.

crispy meringue & cherry-iced cupcakes
Prepare the basic cupcake recipe. Place 4 small meringue shells in a plastic
food storage bag and lightly crush them with a rolling pin. Gently stir into
the icing mixture after adding the food colouring. Swirl onto the cupcakes.

cherry, cherry cupcakes
Prepare the basic cupcake recipe, adding 75 g (3 oz) dried cherries to
the batter.

variations

classic chocolate buttercream cupcakes

see base recipe page 32

white & plain chocolate buttercream cupcakes
Prepare the basic cupcake recipe, stirring 3 tablespoons mixed plain
chocolate chips and white chocolate chips into the creamed batter.

macadamia nut-iced buttercream cupcakes
Prepare the basic cupcake recipe. Lightly toast 60 g (2½ oz) macadamia nuts
and chop finely. Stir the macadamia nuts into the icing mixture after adding
the sugar.

orange & plain chocolate buttercream cupcakes
Prepare the basic cupcake recipe, substituting 1 tablespoon orange zest for
the vanilla essence.

mocha buttercream cupcakes
Prepare the basic cupcake recipe. For the icing, substitute 1 tablespoon
freshly brewed dark coffee for 1 tablespoon of cream.

soured cream chocolate cupcakes
Prepare the basic cupcake recipe, substituting soured cream for the
buttermilk in the cupcakes.

apple sauce & cinnamon cupcakes

see base recipe page 34

apple sauce & pear cupcakes
Prepare the basic cupcake recipe. Substitute 1 ripe and firm, medium pear for the apple. Lay slices on top of each cupcake and sprinkle with sugar.

apple sauce & warm caramel cupcakes
Prepare the basic cupcake recipe. To make a caramel topping, place 200 g (7 oz) caramels in a medium pan with 3 tablespoons evaporated milk. Heat gently, stirring until all the caramels have melted. Prick the top of the cupcakes with a toothpick and spoon the melted caramel over the cooled cakes. Then lay slices of apple on top of each cupcake.

apple sauce & brandy drizzle cupcakes
Prepare the basic cupcake recipe. To make the drizzle, combine 4 tablespoons apple brandy with 3 tablespoons sugar in a medium pan. Simmer gently for 5 minutes, then spoon over the cupcakes. Then lay slices of apple on top of each cupcake.

variations

peanut butter cupcakes

see base recipe page 36

peanut butter & jam cupcakes
Prepare the basic cupcake recipe. When the cupcakes have cooled, use a
sharp knife to slice off the tops. Using a teaspoon, hollow out a small hole
in the top of each cupcake. Spoon ½ teaspoon strawberry or raspberry jam
into the small hole. Place the top back on the cupcake and ice.

chocolate peanut butter cupcakes
Prepare the basic cupcake recipe. Add 100 g (3½ oz) plain chocolate chips to
the batter.

peanut butter cupcakes with fudge icing
Prepare the basic cupcake recipe. For the icing, substitute smooth
peanut butter for the crunchy. Add 2 tablespoons Dutch-process
cocoa powder to the icing mixture after adding the milk.

peanut butter bar cupcakes
Prepare the basic cupcake recipe. When the cupcakes have cooled, use a
sharp knife to slice off the tops. Using a teaspoon, hollow out a small hole
in the top of each cupcake. Spoon ½ teaspoon chopped peanut chocolate
bar into the small hole. Place the top back on the cupcake and ice.

variations

poppy seed cupcakes with lemon drizzle

see base recipe page 37

poppy seed cupcakes with orange & lemon drizzle
Prepare the basic cupcake recipe using $1/2$ tablespoon orange zest and
$1/2$ tablespoon lemon zest. To make the drizzle, use 2 tablespoons lemon juice
and 2 tablespoons orange juice.

poppy seed & blueberry cupcakes with lime drizzle
Prepare the basic cupcake recipe. After creaming the batter, stir in 100 g
($3^1/2$ oz) blueberries, and substitute 1 tablespoon finely grated lime zest for
the lemon zest.

poppy seed & cranberry cupcakes with lemon drizzle
Prepare the basic cupcake recipe. After creaming the batter, stir in 100 g
($3^1/2$ oz) dried chopped cranberries.

almond & poppy seed cupcakes with almond drizzle
Prepare the basic cupcake recipe, substituting 1 teaspoon almond essence
for the lemon zest. For the drizzle, substitute 1 teaspoon almond essence
plus 3 tablespoons milk in place of the lemon juice.

variations

madeleines

see base recipe page 39

cassis-iced madeleines

Prepare the basic recipe. For the icing, substitute 4 tablespoons cassis liqueur for the lemon juice, and proceed as main recipe.

chocolate madeleines

Prepare the basic recipe. Substitute 2 tablespoons Dutch-process cocoa powder for 2 tablespoons of the flour.

vanilla madeleines

Prepare the basic recipe. Add 1 teaspoon vanilla essence to the eggs and sugar before creaming the batter. Add 1 teaspoon vanilla essence to the sugar, butter, salt and orange zest before creaming the icing.

orange madeleines

Prepare the basic cupcake recipe, substituting orange zest for lemon.

variations

banana cupcakes

see base recipe page 40

chocolate chip & banana cupcakes

Prepare the basic cupcake recipe. Stir in 100 g (3½ oz) plain chocolate chips along with the mashed bananas.

cinnamon & oat-topped banana cupcakes

Prepare the basic cupcake recipe, omitting the icing. Place 3 tablespoons caster sugar, 1 teaspoon cinnamon, 2 tablespoons softened unsalted butter, 4 tablespoons porridge oats and 1 tablespoon flour in a medium bowl. Mix until well combined. Sprinkle a little over the cupcakes before baking them.

walnut & cinnamon-iced banana cupcakes

Prepare the basic cupcake recipe. Add 3 tablespoons chopped walnuts and 1 teaspoon cinnamon to the icing after creaming it.

blueberry & banana cupcakes

Prepare the basic cupcake recipe. Stir in 60 g (2 oz) dried blueberries along with the mashed bananas.

fragrant &
spiced cupcakes

Exotic and unexpected flavours make these

cupcakes a culinary adventure. Unusual pairings –

pistachio and rosewater, fig and vanilla, cardamom

and orange – abound.

carnation cupcakes

see variations page 72

Cooking with flowers goes back centuries. You can find old recipes for flower water, jellies, jams and yes, cupcakes!

for the cupcakes
225 g (8 oz) unsalted butter, softened
225 g (8 oz) caster sugar
225 g (8 oz) self-raising flour
4 eggs
1 tsp vanilla essence

for the icing
200 g (7 oz) sugar
2 tbsp lemon juice
3 dozen red, pink or striped carnations

Preheat the oven to 175°C (350°F / Gas mark 4). Place 18 paper baking cases in muffin tins. Combine all the cupcake ingredients in a large bowl and beat with an electric whisk until smooth and pale, about 2 to 3 minutes. Spoon the batter into the cases. Bake for 20 minutes. Remove tins from the oven and cool for 5 minutes. Then remove the cupcakes and cool on a rack.

To make the icing, sieve the icing sugar into a medium bowl. Slowly add the lemon juice, stirring until the icing holds its shape. Spread the icing onto the cooled cupcakes. Snip the stems off the carnation flowers and place a flower in the centre of each cupcake.

Store without icing in an airtight container for up to 3 days, or freeze in an airtight container for up to 3 months.

Makes 1¹/₂ dozen

chai cupcakes

see variations page 73

Chai is a spiced Indian tea made with frothy warm milk – almost like an Indian cappuccino! This cupcake captures its light, spicy flavour.

for the cupcakes
225 g (8 oz) self-raising flour
1/4 tsp baking powder
pinch of salt
1 tbsp chai tea powder
60 g (2 1/2 oz) unsalted butter, softened
150 g (5 oz) light brown sugar
2 egg whites
150 ml (5 fl oz) buttermilk

for the icing
200 g (7 oz) cream cheese, softened
175 g (6 oz) icing sugar, sieved
1 tbsp lemon juice
1 tsp vanilla essence

Preheat the oven to 175°C (350°F / Gas mark 4). Place 12 baking cases in a muffin tin. In a medium bowl, mix the flour, baking powder, salt and chai powder. In a separate bowl, beat the butter and sugar until smooth. Add the egg whites slowly, beating well. Slowly add the flour mixture, and finally the buttermilk. Mix until combined. Spoon the batter into the cases. Bake for 20 minutes. Remove tin from the oven and cool for 5 minutes. Then remove the cupcakes and cool on a rack. To make the icing, mix the cream cheese and icing sugar together in a medium bowl and beat until soft and light. Add the lemon and vanilla, and beat until smooth. Spoon the icing over the cupcakes.

Store without icing in an airtight container for up to 3 days, or freeze for up to 3 months.

Makes 1 dozen

fennel cupcakes

see variations page 74

Lightly crushed fennel seeds give this cupcake a sweet licorice flavour. In India, they are chewed after meals to refresh the breath.

for the cupcakes
225 g (8 oz) unsalted butter, softened
225 g (8 oz) caster sugar
225 g (8 oz) self-raising flour
4 eggs
1 tsp fennel seeds, finely crushed

for the icing
200 g (7 oz) cream cheese, softened
175 g (6 oz) icing sugar, sieved
1 tbsp licorice-flavoured liqueur
1 tsp vanilla essence
1 tsp fennel seeds, lightly crushed

Preheat the oven to 175°C (350°F / Gas mark 4). Place 18 paper baking cases in muffin tins. Combine all the cupcake ingredients in a medium bowl and beat with an electric whisk until smooth and pale, about 2 to 3 minutes. Spoon the batter into the cases. Bake for 20 minutes. Remove tins from the oven and cool for 5 minutes. Then remove the cupcakes and cool on a rack.

To make the icing, combine the cream cheese and icing sugar, and beat briskly until soft and creamy. Add the liqueur and vanilla, and stir well. Swirl onto the top of the cupcakes, and decorate with the fennel seeds.

Store without icing for up to 3 days in an airtight container, or freeze for 3 months.

Makes 1¹/₂ dozen

rhubarb & ginger cupcakes

see variations page 75

The combination of rhubarb and ginger is magnificent. It is believed that rhubarb originated in China, where it was used for its medicinal properties.

for the cupcakes
225 g (8 oz) unsalted butter, softened
225 g (8 oz) caster sugar
225 g (8 oz) self-raising flour
4 eggs
1 tsp vanilla essence
150 g (5 oz) cooked rhubarb

for the icing
200 g (7 oz) cream cheese, softened
175 g (6 oz) icing sugar, sieved
1 tbsp lime juice
$^1/_2$ tsp ground ginger
$1^1/_2$ tbsp roughly chopped crystallised ginger

Preheat the oven to 200°C (400°F / Gas mark 6). Place 18 paper baking cases in muffin tins. Combine all the cupcake ingredients, except the rhubarb, in a medium bowl and beat with an electric whisk until smooth and pale, about 2 to 3 minutes. Spoon the batter into the cups. Bake for 20 minutes. Remove tins from the oven and cool for 5 minutes. Then remove the cupcakes and cool on a rack. Hollow out a small hole in each cake and fill with 1 teaspoon rhubarb.

For the icing, combine the cream cheese and icing sugar, and beat briskly until soft and creamy. Add the lime juice, ground ginger and crystallised ginger and mix well. Spoon onto the cupcakes. Store without icing in an airtight container for up to 3 days, or freeze for up to 3 months.

Makes 1$^1/_2$ dozen

lavender & honey cupcakes

see variations page 76

The marriage of lavender and honey is truly wonderful. If you can find lavender honey, it will enhance the flavour even more.

for the cupcakes
225 g (8 oz) unsalted butter, softened
225 g (8 oz) caster sugar
225 g (8 oz) self-raising flour
4 eggs
1 tsp vanilla essence

for the icing
200 g (7 oz) cream cheese, softened
175 g (6 oz) icing sugar, sieved
75 g (3 oz) honey
blue food colouring
2 tbsp dried lavender flowers

Preheat the oven to 200°C (400°F / Gas mark 6). Place 18 baking cases in muffin tins. Combine all the cupcake ingredients in a medium bowl and beat with an electric whisk until smooth and pale, about 2 to 3 minutes. Spoon the batter into the cases. Bake for 20 minutes. Remove tins from the oven and cool for 5 minutes. Then remove the cupcakes and cool on a rack.

For the icing, beat the cream cheese and icing sugar in a medium bowl with an electric whisk, until light and creamy. Beat in the honey and a few drops of the food colouring. Stir in half of the lavender flowers. Spread the icing onto the cupcakes and sprinkle with the reserved lavender flowers.

Store without icing in an airtight container for up to 3 days, or freeze for up to 3 months.

Makes 1½ dozen

hummingbird cupcakes with marmalade icing

see variations page 77

The hummingbird cake is a classic recipe from the American South.

for the cupcakes
125 g (4¹/₂ oz) plain flour
1 tsp baking powder
¹/₂ tsp cinnamon
125 g (4¹/₂ oz) caster sugar
115 ml (4 fl oz) sunflower oil
2 eggs
150 g (5 oz) mashed bananas
1¹/₂ tbsp grated orange zest

60 g (2¹/₂ oz) grated carrot
100 g (3¹/₂ oz) tinned pineapple, crushed
60 g (2¹/₂ oz) desiccated coconut

for the icing
115 g (4 oz) unsalted butter, softened
150 g (5 oz) icing sugar, sieved
2 tbsp freshly squeezed orange juice
2 tbsp orange marmalade

Preheat the oven to 175°C (350°F / Gas mark 4). Place 12 baking cases in a muffin tin. In a medium bowl, sieve the flour, baking powder and cinnamon. In a large bowl, cream the sugar and oil with an electric whisk until light and fluffy. Beat in the eggs slowly, then stir in the dry ingredients in 3 batches. Add the rest of the ingredients, and stir until combined. Spoon the batter into the cases. Bake for 25 minutes. Remove tin from the oven and cool for 5 minutes. Then remove the cupcakes and cool on a rack. To make the icing, beat the butter in a medium bowl. Add the sugar and orange juice, and beat smooth. Add marmalade or save for garnish. Spread or dollop icing onto cupcakes and garnish with marmalade if desired. Store without icing in an airtight container for up to 3 days, or freeze for up to 3 months.

Makes 1 dozen

pistachio & rosewater cupcakes

see variations page 78

Rosewater is a delicate, sweet flavouring made by steeping rose petals in water, oil or alcohol. Try to use unsalted pistachios in this recipe.

for the cupcakes
225 g (8 oz) unsalted butter, softened
225 g (8 oz) caster sugar
225 g (8 oz) self-raising flour
2 tsp baking powder
4 eggs
1 tsp rosewater

for the icing
200 g (7 oz) cream cheese
175 g (6 oz) icing sugar, sieved
2 tbsp rosewater
3 tbsp chopped pistachios

Preheat the oven to 175°C (350°F / Gas mark 4). Place 18 paper baking cases in muffin tins. Combine all the cupcake ingredients in a medium bowl and beat with an electric whisk until smooth and pale, about 2 to 3 minutes. Spoon the batter into the cases. Bake for 20 minutes. Remove tins from the oven and cool for 5 minutes. Then remove the cupcakes and cool on a rack.

For the icing, combine the cream cheese and icing sugar, and beat with an electric mixer until soft and creamy. Add the rosewater and stir well. Add pistachios, or save them for garnish. Swirl icing onto the top of the cupcakes and garnish with pistachios if desired. Store without icing for up to 3 days in an airtight container, or freeze for up to 3 months.

Makes 1¹/₂ dozen

orange & armagnac cupcakes

see variations page 79

For adults only! These cupcakes would be ideal on a cold winter night.

for the cupcakes
225 g (8 oz) unsalted butter, softened
225 g (8 oz) caster sugar
225 g (8 oz) self-raising flour
4 eggs
2 tbsp Armagnac

for the icing
200 g (7 oz) cream cheese, softened
175 g (6 oz) icing sugar, sieved
1 tsp orange essence
1¹/₂ tbsp grated orange zest

Preheat the oven to 175°C (350°F / Gas mark 4). Place 18 paper baking cases in muffin tins. Combine all the cupcake ingredients in a medium bowl and beat with an electric whisk until smooth and pale, about 2 to 3 minutes. Spoon the batter into the cases. Bake for 20 minutes. Remove tins from the oven and cool for 5 minutes.

With a skewer or toothpick, poke holes in the tops of the cupcakes, then drizzle lightly with Armagnac. Then remove the cupcakes and cool on a rack. To make the icing, beat the cream cheese in a bowl with an electric mixer until light and fluffy. Beat in the icing sugar for 1 to 2 minutes, then beat in the orange essence and zest until smooth and light. Spread the icing on the cupcakes. Store without icing for up to 2 days in an airtight container, or freeze for up to 3 months.

Makes 1¹/₂ dozen

spiced soured cream cupcakes

see variations page 80

The hearty flavour of these cupcakes is perfect for bonfire parties and autumn picnics.

for the cupcakes
190 g (6¹/₂ oz) plain flour
1 tsp baking powder
2 tsp cinnamon
1 tsp mixed spice
¹/₄ tsp nutmeg
2 eggs
175 ml (6 fl oz) soured cream
175 g (6 oz) light brown sugar

3 tbsp sultanas
3 tbsp chopped pecans

for the icing
200 g (7 oz) cream cheese, softened
115 g (4 oz) unsalted butter, softened
175 g (6 oz) icing sugar, sieved
1 tbsp grated orange zest
2 tbsp orange juice

Preheat the oven to 175°C (350°F / Gas mark 4). Place 18 paper baking cases in muffin tins. Sieve the dry ingredients into a medium bowl and put aside. In a large bowl, beat the eggs and soured cream with an electric mixer. Add the sugar and mix well. Then add the dry ingredients in 3 batches, and mix until smooth. Stir in the raisins and pecans. Spoon the batter into the cases.

Bake for 20 minutes until firm. Remove tins from the oven and cool for 5 minutes. Then remove the cupcakes and cool on a rack. To make the icing, beat the cream cheese and butter together with an electric mixer, until light and fluffy. Add the icing sugar and beat until creamy. Beat in the orange zest and the juice. Spread the icing on the cupcakes.

Store without icing in an airtight container for up to 3 days, or freeze for up to 3 months.

Makes 1¹/₂ dozen

cardamom & orange cupcakes

see variations page 81

Cardamom has a pungent aroma and is often used in Indian cooking to flavour curries.

for the cupcakes
225 g (8 oz) unsalted butter, softened
225 g (8 oz) caster sugar
225 g (8 oz) self-raising flour
4 eggs
1 tsp ground cardamom
1 tsp orange essence

for the icing
250 g (9 oz) icing sugar, sieved
115 g (4 oz) unsalted butter, softened
50 ml (2 fl oz) soured cream
1½ tbsp grated orange zest
1 tsp orange essence
36 cardamom pods (for decoration only)

Preheat the oven to 175°C (350°F / Gas mark 4). Place 18 paper baking cases in muffin tins. Combine all the cupcake ingredients in a medium bowl and beat with an electric whisk until smooth and pale, about 2 to 3 minutes. Spoon the batter into the cases. Bake in the oven for 20 minutes. Remove tins from the oven and cool for 5 minutes. Then remove the cupcakes and cool on a rack.

To make the icing, beat the icing sugar, butter, soured cream, orange zest and orange essence with an electric whisk until smooth. Spread the icing on the cupcakes and top each with 2 cardamom pods. Store without icing for up to 2 days in an airtight container, or freeze for up to 3 months.

Makes 1½ dozen

variations

carnation cupcakes

see base recipe page 57

iced flower cupcakes
Prepare the basic cupcake recipe. To prepare the iced flowers, put an egg white in a small bowl and some caster sugar in another small bowl. Take a selection of flower petals (roses and pansies work well) and brush with egg white on both sides. Dust the petals with the sugar, place on a tray, and leave in a cool dry place to dry and stiffen. Lay on top of the iced cupcakes.

rose cupcakes
Prepare the basic cupcake recipe. Substitute 2 dozen rose petals for the carnations.

citrus cream carnation cupcakes
Prepare the basic cupcake recipe. To make a citrus cream icing, combine 100 g (3½ oz) cream cheese with 2 teaspoons orange and lemon zest in a small bowl. Stir in 3 tablespoons icing sugar, spread onto the cupcakes and garnish with the carnations.

jordan almond cupcakes
Prepare the basic cupcake recipe, substituting almond essence for vanilla. Substitute pastel-coloured Jordan almonds for the carnations.

variations

chai cupcakes

see base recipe page 58

chocolate chip & chai cupcakes
Prepare the basic cupcake recipe, stirring in 100 g (3½ oz) plain chocolate chips after adding the buttermilk.

cinnamon & orange chai cupcakes
Prepare the basic cupcake recipe, adding 2 teaspoons cinnamon to the dry ingredients. Add 1 tablespoon grated orange zest along with the buttermilk.

white chocolate & vanilla chai cupcakes
Prepare the basic cupcake recipe. Add 100 g (3½ oz) white chocolate chips and 1 teaspoon vanilla essence after adding the buttermilk.

chai cupcakes with lemon drizzle
Prepare the basic cupcake recipe. Omit the cream cheese and whisk the icing sugar, lemon juice and vanilla together and drizzle over the cupcakes.

malted milk cupcakes
Prepare the basic cupcake recipe, substituting malted milk powder for the chai. For the icing, substitute 2 tablespoons chocolate syrup for the lemon juice and decorate the cupcakes with chocolate-covered malted milk balls.

variations

fennel cupcakes

see base recipe page 60

fennel & orange cupcakes
Prepare the basic cupcake recipe. Add 1 tablespoon finely grated orange zest to the cupcake mixture. For the icing, substitute 1 teaspoon orange essence for the vanilla.

fennel & almond cupcakes
Prepare the basic cupcake recipe, adding 4 tablespoons chopped blanched almonds after mixing the cupcake batter.

fennel & pink pepper cupcakes
Prepare the basic cupcake recipe. For the icing, omit the vanilla essence and instead add 1 teaspoon finely crushed pink peppercorns.

cardamom cupcakes
Prepare the basic cupcake recipe, substituting crushed cardamom seeds for the fennel and orange-flavoured liqueur for the licorice-flavoured liqueur.

poppy seed & amaretto cupcakes
Prepare the basic cupcake recipe, substituting poppy seeds for the fennel and almond-flavoured liqueur for the licorice-flavoured liqueur.

rhubarb & ginger cupcakes

see base recipe page 61

rhubarb, cinnamon & ginger cupcakes
Prepare the basic cupcake recipe. Add 2 teaspoons cinnamon to the cupcake mixture before stirring the batter.

rhubarb, custard & ginger cupcakes
Prepare the basic cupcake recipe. Slice the cupcakes horizontally and spread 1 tablespoon custard (or prepared vanilla pudding) onto the base. Pop the top back on and smother with the ginger icing.

sultana, rhubarb & ginger cupcakes
Prepare the basic cupcake recipe. After mixing the batter, add 60 g (2¹/₂ oz) sultanas.

lemony rhubarb cupcakes
Prepare the basic cupcake recipe, substituting lemon zest for the vanilla essence. In the icing, substitute lemon juice for lime juice and omit the ground and crystallised ginger.

orange–rhubarb cupcakes
Prepare the basic cupcake recipe, substituting orange zest for the vanilla essence. In the icing, substitute orange juice for lime juice and finely chopped crystallised orange peel for the ground and crystallised ginger.

variations

lavender & honey cupcakes

see base recipe page 63

dark chocolate & lavender cupcakes
Prepare the basic cupcake recipe. After mixing the batter, fold in 100 g
(3½ oz) plain dark chocolate chips.

lavender–blueberry cupcakes
Prepare the basic cupcake recipe, substituting lemon zest for vanilla and
adding 225 g (8 oz) dried blueberries to the cupcake batter after creaming.
For the icing, substitute 2 tablespoons lemon juice for the honey and 100 g
(4 oz) fresh blueberries for the lavender flowers.

lavender & orange flower cream cupcakes
Prepare the basic cupcake recipe. To make the icing, combine 3 tablespoons
orange flower water with the cream cheese and icing sugar. Add the honey.
Beat well and stir in the lavender flowers.

lemon–lavender cupcakes
Prepare the basic cupcake recipe, substituting lemon zest for the vanilla
essence. To make the icing, add 1 teaspoon lemon zest to the cream cheese
and icing sugar. Add the honey. Beat well and stir in the lavender flowers.

variations

hummingbird cupcakes with marmalade icing

see base recipe page 64

macadamia hummingbird cupcakes with marmalade icing
Prepare the basic cupcake recipe adding 100 g (3½ oz) chopped macadamia
nuts after mixing in the eggs.

hummingbird cupcakes with figs
Prepare the basic cupcake recipe, substituting 90 g (3¼ oz) chopped dried
figs for the pineapple.

hummingird cupcakes with lemon icing
Prepare the basic cupcake recipe. To make the icing, substitute 2 tablespoons
lemon juice for the orange juice, and 2 tablespoons lemon curd for
the marmalade.

hummingbird cupcakes with pineapple icing
Prepare the basic cupcake recipe. To make the icing, substitute 2 tablespoons
lemon juice for the orange juice, and 45 g (1½ oz) crushed pineapple for
the marmalade.

black walnut hummingbird cupcakes with marmalade icing
Prepare the basic cupcake, adding 60 g (2 oz) finely ground black walnuts
to the batter after creaming.

variations

pistachio & rosewater cupcakes

see base recipe page 67

pomegranate & rosewater cupcakes
Prepare the basic cupcake recipe. For the icing, add 3 tablespoons pomegranate seeds after combining the cream cheese and icing sugar.

walnut & rosewater cupcakes
Prepare the basic cupcake recipe. For the icing, substitute 3 tablespoons chopped walnuts for the pistachios.

almond & rosewater cupcakes
Prepare the basic cupcake recipe. For the icing, substitute 3 tablespoons toasted almonds for the pistachios.

pistachio & orange flower water cupcakes
Prepare the basic cupcake recipe, substituting orange flower water for the rosewater. For the icing, substitute 1 tablespoon orange flower water for the rosewater.

pistachio & amaretto cupcakes
Prepare the basic cupcake recipe, substituting 1 tablespoon Amaretto for the 1 teaspoon rosewater.

variations

orange & armagnac cupcakes

see base recipe page 68

orange, chocolate chip & armagnac cupcakes
Prepare the basic cupcake recipe, adding 100 g (3½ oz) plain chocolate chips after combining the rest of the cupcake ingredients.

almond & amaretto cupcakes
Prepare the basic cupcake recipe, substituting 2 tablespoons Amaretto for the Armagnac. Add 3 tablespoons ground almonds to the cupcake mixture along with the other ingredients. For the icing, add 2 tablespoons chopped almonds, and omit the orange juice and zest.

hazelnut & kahlua cupcakes
Prepare the basic cupcake recipe, substituting 2 tablespoons Kahlua for the Armagnac. Add 3 tablespoons finely chopped hazelnuts to the cupcake mixture along with the other ingredients. For the icing, add 2 tablespoons chopped hazelnuts, and omit the orange juice and zest.

orange, prune & armagnac cupcakes
Prepare the basic cupcake recipe, adding 75 g (3 oz) chopped, pitted prunes after combining the rest of the cupcake ingredients.

variations

spiced soured cream cupcakes

see base recipe page 69

ginger-iced spiced soured cream cupcakes
Prepare the basic cupcake recipe. For the icing, substitute 3 tablespoons chopped crystallised ginger for the orange zest and orange juice.

coffee-iced spiced soured cream cupcakes
Prepare the basic cupcake recipe, but omit the icing. For the icing, mix 2 tablespoons strong coffee and 2 tablespoons malted milk powder until dissolved. Whisk 175 g (6 oz) icing sugar into the coffee mixture until dissolved.

maple & walnut-iced spiced soured cream cupcakes
Prepare the basic cupcake recipe. To make the icing, add ½ teaspoon maple-flavoured essence to the creamed icing sugar, butter and cream cheese. Omit the orange juice and zest. Smear the icing onto the cupcakes and top with 100 g (3½ oz) chopped walnuts.

apple sauce spiced cupcakes
Prepare the basic cupcake recipe, substituting apple sauce for the soured cream.

cardamom & orange cupcakes

see base recipe page 70

coffee & cardamom-iced cupcakes

Prepare the basic cupcake recipe. For the icing, omit the orange zest and essence. Add 2 tablespoons instant coffee granules to 1 teaspoon hot coffee. Stir to dissolve. Stir in 1 tablespoon Kahlua. Set aside to cool. Stir the cooled coffee mixture into the creamed icing sugar, butter and soured cream.

cardamom, custard & orange cupcakes

Prepare the basic cupcake recipe. Slice the cupcakes horizontally and spread 1 tablespoon custard onto the base. Pop the top back on and smother with the orange icing.

cardamom & lemongrass cupcakes

Prepare the basic cupcake recipe. For the icing, add 1 tablespoon finely chopped lemongrass after creaming the other ingredients.

cardamom, ice cream & orange cupcakes

Prepare the basic cupcake recipe. Slice the cupcakes horizontally and place a small scoop of cinnamon ice cream onto the base. Pop the top back on and drizzle with warm caramel ice cream topping.

chocolate
cupcakes

Minted chocolate cupcakes, chocolate chip and

raisin brioches, white chocolate and strawberry

cupcakes – the cupcakes in this chapter will satisfy

your chocolate craving in an instant!

chocolate mud cupcakes

see variations page 103

These cupcakes are so simple to make, you won't hesitate to make another batch!

300 g (10½ oz) plain chocolate chips
300 g (10½ oz) unsalted butter
5 eggs

115 g (4 oz) caster sugar
115 g (4 oz) self-raising flour
2 tbsp Dutch-process cocoa powder, for dusting

Preheat the oven to 160°C (325°F / Gas mark 3). Place 12 paper baking cases in a muffin tin.

In a medium bowl set over a pan of gently simmering water, melt the chocolate and butter together, stirring well. Leave to cool a little.

Beat the eggs and sugar in a large bowl until pale and thick. Fold the flour into the egg mixture and then stir in the melted chocolate and butter until well blended.

Spoon the mixture into the cases and bake for 20 minutes. The cupcakes will be soft and gooey in texture and appearance. Remove tin from the oven and cool for 5 minutes. Then remove the cupcakes from tin. Serve swiftly, dusted with cocoa powder.

Store in the refrigerator in an airtight container for up to 3 days.

Makes 1 dozen

chocolate ice cream cupcakes

see variations page 104

It's best to move these cupcakes from freezer to refrigerator 30 minutes before serving.

for the cupcakes
225 g (8 oz) unsalted butter, softened
225 g (8 oz) caster sugar
225 g (8 oz) self-raising flour
4 tbsp Dutch-process cocoa powder
1 tsp baking powder
4 eggs
1 tsp vanilla essence

for the filling and glaze
175 g (6 oz) chocolate ice cream
100 g (3½ oz) plain chocolate chips
75 ml (3 fl oz) whipping cream

Preheat the oven to 175°C (350°F / Gas mark 4). Place 18 paper baking cases in muffin tins. Combine all the cupcake ingredients in a medium bowl and beat with an electric whisk until smooth and creamy, about 2 to 3 minutes.

Spoon the batter into the cases. Bake for 20 minutes. Remove tins from the oven and cool for 5 minutes. Then remove the cupcakes and cool on a rack. When cool, slice the cupcakes horizontally and spread a little softened ice cream on the bottom slice. Place the top back on the cupcake and freeze. Prepare the glaze by melting the chocolate in a medium bowl over a pan of simmering water, stirring until completely melted. Remove from the heat. Add the cream and stir until well combined. Cool slightly and spoon over the cupcakes. Return to the freezer to set.

Freeze in an airtight container for up to 3 months.

Makes 1½ dozen

white chocolate &
strawberry cupcakes

see variations page 105

Simple yet sophisticated – and perfect for a summer picnic!

for the cupcakes
225 g (8 oz) unsalted butter, softened
225 g (8 oz) caster sugar
225 g (8 oz) self-raising flour
1 tsp baking powder
4 eggs
1 tsp strawberry essence
100 g (3½ oz) white chocolate chips

for the icing
200 g (7 oz) cream cheese, softened
175 g (6 oz) icing sugar, sieved
1 tsp vanilla essence
3 tbsp unsalted butter, softened
3 tbsp chopped fresh strawberries

Preheat the oven to 175°C (350°F / Gas mark 4). Place 18 paper baking cases in muffin tins. Combine the butter, sugar, flour, baking powder, eggs and strawberry essence in a medium bowl. Beat with an electric whisk until light and creamy, about 2 to 3 minutes. Stir in the chocolate chips. Spoon the batter into the cases. Bake for 20 minutes. Remove tins from the oven and cool for 5 minutes. Then remove the cupcakes and cool on a rack. To make the icing, beat the cream cheese, icing sugar, vanilla and butter until smooth and creamy. Stir in the chopped strawberries. Spread icing on top of the cupcakes.

Store without icing in an airtight container for up to 2 days, or freeze for up to 3 months.

Makes 1½ dozen

chocolate & chilli cupcakes

see variations page 106

The Spanish *conquistadors* brought chocolate back from Mexico, a fact that inspired this delicious combination of dark chocolate and tingling chilli.

for the cupcakes
225 g (8 oz) unsalted butter, softened
225 g (8 oz) caster sugar
225 g (8 oz) self-raising flour
4 tbsp Dutch-process cocoa powder
1 tsp baking powder
4 eggs
2 tsp chilli powder
100 g (3½ oz) plain dark chocolate chips

for the icing
175 g (6 oz) icing sugar, sieved
50 g (2 oz) Dutch-process cocoa powder
3 tbsp Tia Maria
115 g (4 oz) unsalted butter, softened

Preheat the oven to 175°C (350°F / Gas mark 4). Place 18 paper baking cases in muffin tins. Combine all the cupcake ingredients, except the chocolate chips, in a large bowl and beat with an electric whisk until smooth, about 2 to 3 minutes. Stir in the chocolate chips. Spoon the batter into the cases. Bake for 20 minutes. Remove tins from the oven and cool for 5 minutes. Then remove the cupcakes and cool on a rack.

To make the icing, blend all the ingredients together in a food processor. Spread the icing on the cooled cupcakes.

Store without icing in an airtight container for up to 2 days.

Makes 1½ dozen

white chocolate &
macadamia nut cupcakes

see variations page 107

Technically, white chocolate is not a chocolate, but it tastes just as decadent!

for the cupcakes
225 g (8 oz) unsalted butter, softened
225 g (8 oz) caster sugar
225 g (8 oz) self-raising flour
1 tsp baking powder
1/2 tsp salt
4 eggs
1 tsp vanilla essence
100 g (3 1/2 oz) white chocolate chips

for the icing
200 g (7 oz) white chocolate chips
5 tbsp milk
175 g (6 oz) icing sugar, sieved
3 tbsp chopped, toasted macadamia nuts

Preheat the oven to 175°C (350°F / Gas mark 4). Place 18 paper baking cases in muffin tins. Combine all the cupcake ingredients, except the chocolate chips, in a large bowl and beat with an electric whisk until smooth and pale, about 2 to 3 minutes. Stir in the chocolate chips. Spoon the batter into the cases. Bake for 20 minutes. Remove tins from the oven and cool for 5 minutes. Then remove the cupcakes and cool on a rack. To make the icing, melt the chocolate and milk in a medium bowl over a pan of simmering water, stirring frequently. Remove from the heat and beat in the icing sugar until smooth. Spread over the cupcakes and sprinkle with the nuts. Store without icing in an airtight container for up to 2 days.

Makes 1 1/2 dozen

chocolate fudge-iced cupcakes

see variations page 108

This fudge icing is bound to bring even the mildest chocaholics to their knees!

for the cupcakes
225 g (8 oz) unsalted butter, softened
225 g (8 oz) caster sugar
225 g (8 oz) self-raising flour
1 tsp baking powder
1/2 tsp salt
4 eggs
1 tsp vanilla essence

for the icing
100 g (31/2 oz) dark chocolate, roughly chopped
2 tbsp milk
50 g (2 oz) unsalted butter
100 g (31/2 oz) icing sugar, sieved

Preheat the oven to 175°C (350°F / Gas mark 4). Place 18 paper baking cases into muffin tins. Combine all the cupcake ingredients in a medium bowl and beat with an electric whisk until smooth and pale, about 2 to 3 minutes. Spoon the batter into the cases. Bake for 20 minutes. Remove the tins from the oven and cool for 5 minutes. Remove the cupcakes and cool on the rack.

To make the icing, gently heat the chocolate, milk and butter in a small, heavy-based saucepan, stirring until melted. Remove from the heat and beat in the icing sugar. Swirl the icing onto the cooled cupcakes.

Store without icing in an airtight container for up to 3 days, or freeze for up to 3 months.

Makes 11/2 dozen

devil's food cupcakes

see variations page 109

These cupcakes are incredibly rich and moist delights!

for the cupcakes
225 g (8 oz) self-raising flour
1 tsp baking powder
225 g (8 oz) light brown sugar
225 g (8 oz) unsalted butter, softened
2 eggs, separated
100 g (3¹/₂ oz) plain chocolate, melted
1 tsp vanilla essence
115 ml (4 fl oz) milk

for the icing
115 g (4 oz) unsalted butter, softened
1 tbsp milk
115 g (4 oz) plain dark chocolate, melted
1 tsp vanilla essence
100 g (3¹/₂ oz) icing sugar, sieved

Preheat the oven to 175°C (350°F / Gas mark 4). Place 18 paper baking cases into muffin tins. Sieve the flour and baking powder and set aside. In a medium bowl, cream the sugar and butter. Add the egg yolks and beat well. Add the melted chocolate and vanilla, mixing well. Add the flour and milk alternately, beating well with each addition. Beat the egg whites in a medium bowl until soft peaks form, and gently fold them into the batter. Spoon the batter into the cases. Bake for 20 minutes. Remove tins from the oven and cool for 5 minutes. Then remove the cupcakes and cool on a rack. To make the icing, cream the butter in a medium bowl. Beat in the milk until smooth. Stir in the chocolate and vanilla. Beat in the icing sugar until thick and creamy. Spread over the cupcakes.

Store without icing in an airtight container for up to 2 days, or freeze for up to 3 months.

Makes 1¹/₂ dozen

choc 'n' cherry cupcakes

see variations page 110

The classic German dessert 'Black Forest Gâteau' was the inspiration for this cupcake.

for the cupcakes
225 g (8 oz) self-raising flour
4 tbsp Dutch-process cocoa powder
1 tsp baking powder
225 g (8 oz) caster sugar
225 g (8 oz) unsalted butter, softened
4 eggs
90 g (3¼ oz) chopped cherries
2 tbsp kirsch (or other cherry-flavoured liqueur)

for the topping
200 ml (7 fl oz) whipping cream
3 tbsp icing sugar, sieved
12 whole cherries
100 g (3½ oz) dark chocolate bar

Preheat the oven to 160°C (325°F / Gas mark 3). Place 18 paper baking cases in muffin tins. In a medium bowl, sieve together the flour, cocoa and baking powder. Set aside. Cream the sugar and butter in a large bowl until smooth. Add the eggs one at a time, beating well with each addition. Add the flour mixture and the cherries, and stir until well combined. Spoon the batter into the cases. Bake for 20 minutes. Remove tins from the oven and cool for 5 minutes. Pour a little kirsch over each cupcake. Remove the cupcakes from the tins and cool on a rack.

For the topping, whip the cream and icing sugar together until slightly stiff. Using a vegetable peeler, shave curls of chocolate from the bar. Garnish the cupcakes with a dollop of cream. Place a cherry in the centre and chocolate around it. Store without icing in an airtight container for up to 3 days.

Makes 1½ dozen

mint chocolate cupcakes

see variations page 111

Mint is a versatile herb that complements both sweet and savoury dishes.

for the cupcakes
225 g (8 oz) self-raising flour
4 tbsp Dutch-process cocoa powder
1 tsp baking powder
225 g (8 oz) caster sugar
225 g (8 oz) unsalted butter, softened
4 eggs
1 tsp mint essence
100 g (3½ oz) plain chocolate chips

for the icing
115 g (4 oz) unsalted butter, softened
225 g (8 oz) icing sugar, sieved
1 tsp mint essence
green food colouring
100 g (3½ oz) plain chocolate chips

Preheat the oven to 160°C (325°F / Gas mark 3). Place 18 paper baking cases into muffin tins. In a medium bowl, sieve together the flour, cocoa and baking powder. Set aside. Beat the sugar and butter together in a large bowl until smooth. Add the eggs one at a time, beating well after each addition. Add the flour mixture gradually, stirring until well combined. Stir in the mint essence and chocolate chips. Spoon the mixture into the cases. Bake for 20 minutes. Remove the tins from the oven and cool for 5 minutes. Then remove the cupcakes and cool on a rack. To make the icing, beat the butter and icing sugar in a small bowl until smooth and creamy. Stir in the mint essence and just enough food colouring to turn the icing a mint green. Ice the cupcakes and decorate with chocolate chips.

Store without icing in an airtight container for up to 3 days, or freeze for up to 3 months.

Makes 1½ dozen

chocolate chip & raisin brioches

see variations page 112

You'll find yourself drawn to the breakfast table by the aroma of these sweet breads, a perfect accompaniment to steaming hot coffee.

$1/2$ tbsp active dried yeast
115 ml (4 fl oz) warm water
1 tsp sugar
275 g (10 oz) plain flour
4 eggs
60 g ($2^1/2$ oz) caster sugar

pinch of salt
115 g (4 oz) unsalted butter, softened
100 g ($3^1/2$ oz) raisins
115 g (4 oz) plain chocolate chips
1 egg, beaten

Combine the yeast, water and the teaspoon of sugar in a large bowl. Stir well and leave in a warm place for 10 minutes. Stir in 100g ($3^1/2$ oz) of the flour until the mixture becomes a smooth paste. Beat the eggs and add them to the yeast mixture. Add the sugar and salt. Stir in the remaining flour, and mix until the dough is soft and slightly sticky. Leave in a warm place, covered with cling film, for 45 minutes or until doubled in bulk. Preheat the oven to 200°C (400°F / Gas mark 6). Grease 12 mini brioche or muffin moulds. Beat the butter, raisins and chocolate chips into the dough. Fill the moulds halfway. Leave in a warm place to rise for about 20 minutes, until the dough has risen to fill about two-thirds of each mould.

Brush each brioche with a little of the beaten egg and bake for 20 minutes. Cool in the moulds for 5 minutes, remove and cool on a rack.

Store in an airtight container for up to 2 days.

Makes 1 dozen

chocolate hazelnut cupcakes

see variations page 113

A timeless combination . . . with very little flour in the mix!

115 g (4 oz) unsalted butter
115 g (4 oz) plain chocolate chips
115 g (4 oz) caster sugar

4 eggs, separated
2 tbsp plain flour
50 g (2 oz) chopped, roasted hazelnuts

Preheat the oven to 160°C (325°F / Gas mark 3). Place 12 paper baking cases in a muffin tin. Melt the butter and chocolate in a medium bowl over a pan of simmering water, stirring until completely melted. Cool slightly.

Beat the sugar and egg yolks in a medium bowl until thick and creamy. Stir the butter and chocolate, flour and hazelnuts into the egg mixture.

In a medium bowl, beat the egg whites to soft peaks, and gently fold into the chocolate mixture. Spoon the batter into the cases. Bake for 20 minutes. Remove tin from the oven and cool for 5 minutes. Then remove the cupcakes and cool on a rack.

Store refrigerated in an airtight container for up to 2 days, or freeze for up to 3 months.

Makes 1 dozen

chocolate orange cupcakes

see variations page 114

Orange essence helps sweeten the bitterness of the chocolate.

for the cupcakes
225 g (8 oz) unsalted butter, softened
225 g (8 oz) caster sugar
225 g (8 oz) self-raising flour
2 tsp baking powder
1 tsp salt
4 eggs
1 tsp orange essence

1 1/2 tbsp grated orange zest
100 g (3 1/2 oz) plain chocolate chips

for the glaze
100 g (3 1/2 oz) plain chocolate chips
75 ml (3 fl oz) whipping cream
1 tsp orange essence

Preheat the oven to 175°C (350°F / Gas mark 4). Place 18 paper baking cases into muffin tins. Combine all the cupcake ingredients, except the chocolate chips, in a large bowl and beat with an electric whisk until smooth and pale, about 2 to 3 minutes. Stir in the chocolate chips. Spoon the batter into the cases. Bake for 20 minutes. Remove tins from the oven and cool for 5 minutes. Then remove the cupcakes and cool on a rack.

For the chocolate glaze, melt the chocolate in a medium bowl over a pan of simmering water, stirring until completely melted. Add the cream and orange essence, and stir until well combined. Cool slightly and pour over the cupcakes. Refrigerate until set.

Store unglazed in an airtight container for up to 2 days, or freeze for up to 3 months.

Makes 1 1/2 dozen

chocolate brownie cupcakes

see variations page 115

Try these warm from the oven, topped with a generous spoonful of vanilla-flavoured whipped cream.

for the cupcakes
125 g (4½ oz) plain chocolate chips
125 g (4½ oz) unsalted butter
2 eggs
300 g (10½ oz) caster sugar
1 tsp vanilla essence
115 g (4 oz) plain flour

for the topping
240 ml (8 fl oz) whipping cream
1 tsp vanilla essence
3 tbsp icing sugar, sieved

Preheat the oven to 160°C (325°F / Gas mark 3). Place 12 paper baking cases in a muffin tin. Melt the chocolate and butter in a medium bowl set over a tin of simmering water, stirring until melted. Set aside to cool. In a medium bowl, beat the eggs, sugar and vanilla until pale and thick. Fold in the chocolate and then the flour, mixing until well combined.

Spoon batter into the cases. Bake for 25 minutes.

Remove tin from the oven and cool for 5 minutes. Then remove the cupcakes and cool on a rack. For the topping, beat the cream in a medium bowl until semi-stiff. Fold in the vanilla and icing sugar. Place a dollop or two on each brownie.

Makes 1 dozen

variations

chocolate mud cupcakes

see base recipe page 83

raspberry mud cupcakes
Prepare the basic cupcake recipe. Stir in 100 g (3½ oz) lightly crushed raspberries to the mixture after adding the melted chocolate.

white chocolate mud cupcakes
Prepare the basic cupcake recipe. Substitute 100 g (3½ oz) white chocolate chips for the plain chocolate chips.

macadamia mud cupcakes
Prepare the basic cupcake recipe. Toast and chop 100 g (3½ oz) macadamia nuts, and stir them in after adding the melted chocolate.

mocha mud cupcakes
Prepare the basic cupcake recipe. Stir in 2 teaspoons instant espresso powder to the mixture after adding the melted chocolate.

chocolate truffle mud cupcakes
Prepare the basic cupcake recipe, substituting finely chopped chocolate truffles for the chocolate chips.

variations

chocolate ice cream cupcakes

see base recipe page 85

vanilla ice cream cupcakes
Prepare the basic cupcake recipe, substituting 175 g (6 oz) vanilla ice cream for the chocolate ice cream.

chocolate chip & mint ice cream cupcakes
Prepare the basic cupcake recipe, substituting 175 g (6 oz) mint chocolate chip ice cream for the chocolate ice cream.

caramel ice cream cupcakes
Prepare the basic cupcake recipe, substituting 175 g (6 oz) caramel swirl ice cream for the chocolate ice cream.

coffee ice cream cupcakes
Prepare the basic cupcake recipe, substituting 175 g (6 oz) coffee ice cream for the chocolate ice cream.

variations

white chocolate & strawberry cupcakes

see base recipe page 87

chocolate, strawberry & black pepper cupcakes
Prepare the basic cupcake recipe, but replace the white chocolate chips with plain chocolate chips. Stir in 1 teaspoon freshly ground black pepper.

balsamic vinegar & strawberry cupcakes
Prepare the basic cupcake recipe, substituting 2 teaspoons sweet balsamic vinegar for the vanilla essence. Omit the white chocolate chips.

white chocolate & raspberry cupcakes
Prepare the basic cupcake recipe, using 150 g (5 oz) fresh or thawed frozen raspberries instead of strawberries.

lemony white chocolate & strawberry cupcakes
Prepare the basic cupcake recipe, adding 1 teaspoon grated lemon zest to the batter.

variations

chocolate & chilli cupcakes

see base recipe page 88

white chocolate & chilli cupcakes
Prepare the basic cupcake recipe, substituting white chocolate chips for the plain chocolate chips.

vodka-iced chocolate & chilli cupcakes
Prepare the basic cupcake recipe. For the icing, substitute 3 tablespoons vodka for the Tia Maria.

orange liqueur-iced chocolate & chilli cupcakes
Prepare the basic cupcake recipe. For the icing, substitute 3 tablespoons Grand Marnier or another orange liqueur for the Tia Maria.

mexican chocolate & chilli cupcakes
Prepare the basic cupcake recipe, substituting finely chopped Mexican chocolate for the plain chocolate chips.

white chocolate & macadamia nut cupcakes

see base recipe page 91

white chocolate, apricot & macadamia nut cupcakes

Prepare the basic cupcake recipe, substituting 50 g (2 oz) finely chopped dried apricots for half the white chocolate chips.

white chocolate & almond cupcakes

Prepare the basic cupcake recipe, substituting 50 g (2 oz) chopped blanched almonds for half the white chocolate chips. For the icing, substitute 3 tablespoons toasted almonds for the macadamia nuts.

white chocolate, cranberry & macadamia nut cupcakes

Prepare the basic cupcake recipe, using only 50 g (2 oz) white chocolate chips and adding 50 g (2 oz) dried cranberries and 1 tablespoon orange zest.

white chocolate, vanilla, butter & macadamia nut cupcakes

Prepare the basic cupcake recipe, substituting vanilla, butter and nut flavouring for vanilla essence and stir 75 g (3 oz) sultanas into the batter.

variations

chocolate fudge-iced cupcakes

see base recipe page 92

smartie fudge-iced cupcakes
Prepare the basic cupcake recipe. For the icing, add 100 g (3½ oz) lightly crushed Smarties to the mixture after creaming the other ingredients.

white chocolate fudge-iced cupcakes
Prepare the basic cupcake recipe. For the icing, substitute 100 g (3½ oz) white chocolate for the plain chocolate, and add 1 teaspoon vanilla essence.

fudge-iced sultana cupcakes
Prepare the basic cupcake recipe, and add 75 g (3 oz) sultanas to the mixture after creaming the batter.

truffle-iced cupcakes
Prepare the basic cupcake recipe. For the icing, substitute chopped chocolate truffles for the plain chocolate.

devil's food cupcakes

see base recipe page 93

coffee-iced devil's food cupcakes
Prepare the basic cupcake recipe. For the icing, mix 1 teaspoon hot coffee with 2 tablespoons coffee granules and stir until dissolved. Leave to cool. Stir the cooled coffee into the chocolate icing.

white chocolate-iced devil's food cupcakes
Prepare the basic cupcake recipe. For the icing, substitute 100 g (3½ oz) melted white chocolate for the plain chocolate.

hazelnut & chocolate-iced devil's food cupcakes
Prepare the basic cupcake recipe. For the icing, add 100 g (3½ oz) chopped toasted hazelnuts after combining the other ingredients.

soured cream devil's food cupcakes
Prepare the basic cupcake recipe, substituting 115 g (4 oz) soured cream for 115 g (4 oz) of the butter.

red devil cupcakes
Prepare the basic cupcake recipe, adding 1 tablespoon red food colouring to the batter.

variations

choc 'n' cherry cupcakes

see base recipe page 94

flaked almond & cherry cupcakes
Prepare the basic cupcake recipe, folding 3 tablespoons toasted flaked almonds to the cream after it has been whipped.

choc & prune cupcakes
Prepare the basic cupcake recipe, substituting 100 g (3½ oz) chopped prunes for the cherries. For the icing, substitute 3 tablespoons chopped prunes for the whole cherries.

choc & blueberry cupcakes
Prepare the basic cupcake recipe, substituting 100 g (3½ oz) crushed blueberries for the cherries. For the icing, substitute 3 tablespoons blueberries for the cherries.

choc & golden cherry cupcakes
Prepare the basic cupcake recipe, substituting yellow or golden sweet cherries for red.

choc & coffee cupcakes
Prepare the basic cupcake recipe, substituting Kahlua for kirsch. For the icing, substitute 100 g (3½ oz) chocolate-covered espresso beans for the cherries.

variations

mint chocolate cupcakes

see base recipe page 96

sultana & mint chocolate cupcakes
Prepare the basic cupcake recipe, adding 100 g (3½ oz) sultanas along with the chocolate chips.

extra minty cupcakes
Prepare the basic cupcake recipe, substituting 100 g (3½ oz) mint chocolate chips for the plain chocolate chips.

orange & mint chocolate cupcakes
Prepare the basic cupcake recipe, substituting 100 g (3½ oz) orange chocolate chunks for the plain chocolate chips.

peppermint chocolate cupcakes
Prepare the basic cupcake recipe, substituting peppermint essence for mint essence. In the icing, omit the food colouring, substitute peppermint essence for mint essence, and use peppermint sweets in place of plain chocolate chips.

chocolate mint geranium cupcakes
Prepare the basic cupcake recipe. For the icing, substitute 3 tablespoons fresh chocolate mint geranium leaves for chocolate chips on top of the cupcakes.

chocolate chip & raisin brioches

see base recipe page 98

saffron, chocolate chip & raisin brioches
Prepare the basic cupcake recipe, adding a pinch of saffron to the
dry ingredients.

white chocolate & macadamia nut brioches
Prepare the basic cupcake recipe, substituting 100 g (3½ oz) white chocolate
chips and 115 g (4 oz) chopped macadamia nuts for the chocolate chips
and raisins.

chocolate & cinnamon brioches
Prepare the basic cupcake recipe, adding 2 teaspoons cinnamon to the flour.

chocolate & dried cherry brioches
Prepare the basic cupcake recipe, substituting dried cherries for raisins.

chocolate chip & banana brioches
Prepare the basic cupcake recipe, substituting 115 g (4 oz) mashed banana
(about 1 banana) for the raisins.

variations

chocolate hazelnut cupcakes

see base recipe page 99

chocolate hazelnut & cranberry cupcakes
Prepare the basic cupcake recipe, adding 3 tablespoons chopped dried
cranberries to the egg mixture.

chocolate hazelnut & orange cupcakes
Prepare the basic cupcake recipe, adding 2 tablespoons finely grated orange
zest to the egg mixture.

chocolate macadamia nut cupcakes
Prepare the basic cupcake recipe, substituting 100 g (3½ oz) toasted and
chopped macadamia nuts for the hazelnuts.

chocolate pecan cupcakes
Prepare the basic cupcake recipe, substituting 100 g (3½ oz) toasted and
chopped pecans for the hazelnuts.

chocolate almond cupcakes
Prepare the basic cupcake recipe, adding 1 teaspoon almond essence and
substituting 100 g (3½ oz) toasted flaked almonds for the hazelnuts.

chocolate orange cupcakes

see base recipe page 100

chocolate orange marshmallow-centred cupcakes
Bake and cool the cupcakes. Slice the top off each cupcake and hollow out a small hole. Push 1 mini marshmallow into the hole. Place the 'lid' back on and ice with the chocolate glaze.

chocolate orange & vanilla custard cupcakes
Bake and cool the cupcakes. Slice the top off each cupcake and hollow out a small hole. Pipe 1 teaspoon vanilla custard into the hole. Replace the 'lid' and ice with the chocolate glaze.

white chocolate & vanilla cupcakes
Prepare the basic cupcake recipe, substituting white chocolate chips for the plain chocolate chips and vanilla essence for the orange essence. Omit the orange zest. Use white chocolate chips for the glaze instead of plain chocolate.

chocolate crystallised orange-centred cupcakes
Bake and cool the cupcakes. Slice the top off each cupcake and hollow out a small hole. Push 1 small piece crystallised orange slice into the hole. Place the 'lid' back on and ice with the chocolate glaze.

chocolate brownie cupcakes

see base recipe page 102

pecan brownie cupcakes
Prepare the basic cupcake recipe. Stir 100 g (3½ oz) chopped pecans into the mixture with the chocolate chips.

dalmatian brownie cupcakes
Prepare the basic cupcake recipe, substituting white chocolate chips for half the quantity of plain chocolate chips.

chocolate fudge-iced brownie cupcakes
Prepare the basic cupcake recipe, and omit the topping. To make the icing, combine 100 g (3½ oz) plain chocolate, 2 tablespoons milk and 50 g (2 oz) unsalted butter in a medium saucepan and stir until the chocolate has melted. Cool slightly and add 3 tablespoons icing sugar. Mix until smooth.

chocolate brownie cupcake sundae
Prepare the basic cupcake recipe. To serve, place a cupcake on each plate. Top with a scoop of ice cream, a drizzle of hot fudge or caramel sauce and a dollop of the vanilla cream topping.

decadent cupcakes

The recipes in this chapter will leave no doubt in your mind that the cupcake is most definitely a grown-up treat. From baked cheesecakes to brioche bread pudding to Florentine cupcakes, this chapter provides luxurious desserts in individual-size portions!

florentine cupcakes

see variations page 136

Savour *la dolce vita* when you bite into these Italian-inspired cupcakes.

for the cupcakes
225 g (8 oz) unsalted butter, softened
225 g (8 oz) caster sugar
225 g (8 oz) self-raising flour
4 eggs
1 tsp vanilla essence

for the topping
3 tbsp slivered almonds
3 tbsp corn flakes
3 tbsp roughly chopped glacé cherries
3 tbsp sultanas
5 tbsp condensed milk
50 g (2 oz) plain chocolate, melted
50 g (2 oz) white chocolate, melted

Preheat the oven to 175°C (350°F / Gas mark 4). Place 18 paper baking cases in muffin tins. Combine all the cupcake ingredients in a large bowl and beat with an electric whisk until smooth and pale, about 2 to 3 minutes. Spoon the batter into the cases. Bake for 20 minutes. Remove tins from the oven and cool for 5 minutes. Then remove the cupcakes and cool on a rack. For the florentine topping, combine all the ingredients except the chocolate in a small bowl. Spoon small teaspoons of the mixture onto greaseproof paper-lined baking trays. Bake for 5 minutes, until golden. Remove from the oven and cool for 1 minute. Remove the florentines from the sheet and crumble. Scatter over the cooled cupcakes and drizzle with the chocolate.

Store in an airtight container for up to 2 days, or freeze for up to 3 months.

Makes 1¹/₂ dozen

strawberries & cream cupcakes

see variations page 137

This recipe is great for lazy summer days when plump, sweet and juicy strawberries are at the height of their season.

for the cupcakes
225 g (8 oz) unsalted butter, softened
225 g (8 oz) caster sugar
225 g (8 oz) self-raising flour
4 eggs
1 tsp vanilla essence

for the topping
350 ml (12 fl oz) whipping cream
4 tbsp icing sugar, sieved
1 tsp vanilla essence
375 g (13 oz) small strawberries, sliced
4 tbsp strawberry jelly
1 tbsp water

Preheat the oven to 175°C (350°F / Gas mark 4). Place 18 paper baking cases in muffin tins. Combine all the cupcake ingredients in a medium bowl and beat with an electric whisk until smooth and pale, about 2 to 3 minutes. Spoon the batter into the cases. Bake for 20 minutes. Remove tins from the oven and cool for 5 minutes. Then remove the cupcakes and cool on a rack.

For the topping, beat the cream, icing sugar and vanilla in a small bowl until soft peaks form. Spoon onto the cupcakes and arrange the strawberries on top. In a small saucepan heat the jelly and water until melted. Brush the mixture on top of the strawberries. Chill until ready to serve.

Store, without topping, in an airtight container in the refrigerator for up to 2 days.

Makes 1½ dozen

baked cheesecakes

see variations page 138

These mouthwatering little cupcakes make stunning individual desserts. Make them ahead of time and all you'll have to do is pop them on a plate when your guests are ready.

125 g (4½ oz) digestive biscuit crumbs
75 g (3 oz) unsalted butter, melted
450 g (1 lb) ricotta cheese
450 g (1 lb) cream cheese, softened

2 tsp vanilla essence
175 g (6 oz) icing sugar, sieved
3 eggs
150 g (5 oz) fresh blueberries

Preheat the oven to 160°C (325°F / Gas mark 3). Place 12 paper baking cases in a muffin tin.

Put the digestive biscuit crumbs into a medium bowl and stir in the butter. Spoon tablespoons of the crumb mixture into the cases, pressing firmly into the bottom. Chill until set.

In a large bowl, beat the ricotta until smooth. Add the cream cheese, vanilla and icing sugar, blending until smooth. Slowly add the eggs, blending well. Spoon the mixture into the cases.

Bake for 25 minutes. Remove tin from oven and cool for 5 minutes. Then remove the cupcakes and cool on a rack. Chill until time to serve. Serve topped with blueberries.

Store covered for up to 2 days in the refrigerator.

Makes 1 dozen

kahlua & orange cupcakes

see variations page 139

The combination of Kahlua and orange is wonderful. It makes a delightful drink, and a scrumptious cupcake, too!

for the cupcakes
225 g (8 oz) unsalted butter, softened
225 g (8 oz) caster sugar
225 g (8 oz) self-raising flour
4 eggs
1 tsp orange essence

for the icing
225 g (8 oz) icing sugar, sieved
115 g (4 oz) unsalted butter, softened
60 ml (2½ fl oz) soured cream
2 tbsp Kahlua
1 tbsp grated orange zest

Preheat the oven to 175°C (350°F / Gas mark 4). Place 18 paper baking cases in muffin tins. Combine all the cupcake ingredients in a medium bowl and beat with an electric whisk until smooth and pale, about 2 to 3 minutes. Spoon the batter into the cases. Bake for 20 minutes. Remove tins from the oven and cool for 5 minutes. Then remove the cupcakes and cool on a rack.

To make the icing, beat the icing sugar and butter in a small bowl until soft and creamy. Beat in the soured cream, Kahlua and orange zest. Swirl onto the cooled cupcakes.

Store without icing in an airtight container for up to 2 days, or freeze for up to 3 months.

Makes 1½ dozen

hot chocolate fondant cupcakes

see variations page 140

These cupcakes are very simple but must be served immediately. You can prepare the ramekins and batter in advance.

for the cupcakes
215 g (7½ oz) plain chocolate,
    broken into pieces
225 g (8 oz) unsalted butter, softened
4 eggs
4 egg yolks
115 g (4 oz) caster sugar
3 tbsp plain flour

for the topping
200 ml (7 fl oz) soured cream
cocoa powder or icing sugar,
    for dusting

Preheat the oven to 190°C (375°F / Gas mark 5). Butter 8 medium-sized ramekins. Dust each with flour, and tap out the excess. Melt the chocolate and butter in a medium bowl over a pan of simmering water. Stir until smooth. Set aside to cool. In a large bowl, beat the eggs, egg yolks and sugar until pale and creamy. Gradually add the melted chocolate, stirring until combined. Stir in the flour. Pour the batter into the prepared ramekins and bake for 15 minutes, or until the tops are set.

Turn out onto serving plates. Top each with a dollop of soured cream, and dust with cocoa powder or icing sugar. Serve immediately.

Makes 8

brioche bread pudding cupcakes

see variations page 141

Try this rich and robust cupcake recipe for an unusual and tasty twist on the classic bread pudding.

for the custard
2 eggs
115 g (4 oz) caster sugar
1 tsp vanilla essence
450 ml (16 fl oz) whipping cream

for the cupcakes
12 thin slices brioche (crusts removed)
50 g (2 oz) unsalted butter
100 g (3½ oz) fresh raspberries

To make the custard, cream the eggs, sugar and vanilla in a small bowl. Add the cream, stir well and put aside.

Preheat the oven to 175°C (350°F / Gas mark 4). Grease 12 small moulds with a little melted butter. Butter both sides of the bread and cut each slice into 12 small triangles. Push 3 triangles of bread into each mould, covering the bottom. Add a layer of raspberries. Pour a layer of custard over the raspberries. Repeat the process until there are four layers of each in each mould.

Place the moulds in a roasting tray. Pour boiling water into the pan until it reaches halfway up the moulds. Bake until golden and firm, about 25 minutes. If the puddings begin to colour too much, cover the pan with kitchen foil.

Turn the puddings out of the moulds and serve warm.

Makes 1 dozen

mini espresso cupcakes

see variations page 142

Making these cupcakes in espresso cups adds a special touch to the end of a meal.

for the cupcakes
175 g (6 oz) plain flour
1½ tsp baking powder
pinch of salt
75 g (3 oz) malted milk powder
50 ml (2 fl oz) dark espresso coffee
225 g (8 oz) caster sugar
2 eggs
115 g (4 oz) unsalted butter, softened

for the icing
225 g (8 oz) unsalted butter, softened
340 g (12 oz) icing sugar, sieved
1 tbsp instant coffee granules
2 tsp hot coffee
1 tsp vanilla essence

Preheat the oven to 175°C (350°F / Gas mark 4). Lightly grease 18 espresso cups (or use muffin papers in a muffin tin). Sieve the flour, baking powder and salt into a medium bowl. Combine the milk powder and coffee in a small bowl. Beat the sugar, eggs and butter in a medium bowl until light and creamy. Add the flour and coffee mixtures alternately to the egg mixture. Spoon the mixture into the cups. Bake for 15 minutes. Remove cups from oven and cool on a rack.

To make the icing, beat the butter and icing sugar in a bowl until soft and creamy. Add the coffee granules to the hot coffee and stir. Beat into the butter and sugar mixture, and then stir in the vanilla. Dollop icing on cooled cupcakes in the espresso cups.

Store without icing for up to 2 days in an airtight container, or freeze for up to 3 months.

Makes 1½ dozen

almond & raspberry friands

see variations page 143

Try using different oval or rectangular-shaped friand pans. They are available from speciality cookware shops. If you can't find a friand pan, a regular muffin tin works fine.

190 g (6½ oz) unsalted butter, softened
100 g (3½ oz) ground almonds
6 egg whites
75 g (3 oz) plain flour

100 g (3½ oz) fresh raspberries
115 g (4 oz) caster sugar
icing sugar for dusting

Preheat the oven to 175°C (350°F / Gas mark 4). Grease 12 small friand tins with a little of the butter. Mix all the ingredients in a large bowl, reserving half the raspberries, until just combined.

Pour the batter into the prepared tins and scatter the remaining raspberries on top. Bake for 25 minutes, until golden and firm.

Remove tins from the oven and cool for 5 minutes. Turn friands out onto a rack and cool completely. Serve dusted with icing sugar.

Store in an airtight container for up to 2 days.

Makes 1 dozen

lime meringue cupcakes

see variations page 144

An unusual take on the classic lemon meringue pie. The cupcakes look great, and taste even better!

for the cupcakes
225 g (8 oz) unsalted butter, softened
225 g (8 oz) caster sugar
225 g (8 oz) self-raising flour
4 eggs
1 tsp vanilla essence

for the filling
75 ml (3 fl oz) lime juice
400-g (14-oz) tin condensed milk

for the meringue
3 egg whites
$^{1}/_{4}$ tsp cream of tartar
75 g (3 oz) granulated sugar

Preheat the oven to 175°C (350°F / Gas mark 4). Place 18 paper baking cases in muffin tins. Place all the cupcake ingredients in a large bowl, and beat with an electric whisk until smooth and pale, about 2 to 3 minutes. Spoon the batter into the cases. Bake for 20 minutes. Remove tins from the oven and cool for 5 minutes. Then remove the cupcakes and cool on a rack.

For the filling, combine the lime juice and condensed milk in a small bowl. Remove the top from each cupcake and hollow out a small hole. Spoon the filling into the hole and replace the top. For the meringue, beat the egg whites and cream of tartar until soft peaks form. Add one-third of the sugar and beat for 1 minute. Repeat until all the sugar has been added. Increase the oven temperature to 230°C (450°F / Gas mark 7). Spoon or pipe the meringue on top of the cupcakes. Bake for 5 minutes until golden. Store for no more than 1 day in an airtight container.

Makes 1$^{1}/_{2}$ dozen

pineapple upside-down cupcakes

see variations page 145

A classic cake scaled down to a cupcake! When turning out the cupcakes, allow the sweet juices of the pineapple to be absorbed into the golden sponge.

for the topping
570 g (1 lb 4 oz) pineapple chunks
125 g (4½ oz) unsalted butter, melted
150 g (5 oz) brown sugar

for the cupcakes
225 g (8 oz) unsalted butter, softened
225 g (8 oz) caster sugar
225 g (8 oz) self-raising flour
4 eggs
1 tsp vanilla essence

Preheat the oven to 175°C (350°F / Gas mark 4). Grease two 12-cup muffin tins with butter, and dust with a little flour, tapping out the excess. In the bottom of each cup, drizzle 1 tablespoon melted butter, 1 tablespoon pineapple and 1 tablespoon brown sugar.

Place all the cupcake ingredients in a large bowl and beat with an electric whisk until smooth and pale, about 2 to 3 minutes. Spoon the batter on top of the pineapple mixture in each cup. Bake for 25 minutes. Remove tins from the oven and cool for 10 minutes.

Turn out the cupcakes onto dessert plates, and serve warm with double cream if desired.

Store in an airtight container for up to 2 days.

Makes 2 dozen

little caramel cupcakes

see variations page 146

These delightful cupcakes contain a rich and gooey caramel surprise. They are an ideal companion for a cup of Earl Grey tea.

115 g (4 oz) unsalted butter, softened
150 g (5 oz) brown sugar
2 eggs, lightly beaten
2 tbsp instant coffee granules

1 tbsp boiling water
300 g (10½ oz) self-raising flour
115 ml (4 fl oz) milk
125 g (4½ oz) soft caramels

Preheat the oven to 175°C (350°F / Gas mark 4). Place 12 paper baking cases in a muffin tin.

In a medium bowl, beat the butter and sugar until pale and creamy. Add the eggs slowly. In a small bowl, dissolve the coffee in the water. Beat the coffee into the butter mixture. Add the flour and milk, and beat until well combined.

Spoon the mixture into the cases. Push a couple of the caramels into the centre of each cupcake, and place them in the oven.

Bake for 20 minutes. Cool for 5 minutes in the pan. Turn onto a plate and serve while warm.

Makes 1 dozen

sticky toffee pudding cupcake

see variations page 147

This is an old classic British pudding that has recently enjoyed a bit of a renaissance.

for the cupcakes
175 g (6 oz) self-raising flour
100 g (3½ oz) brown sugar
115 g (4 fl oz) milk
1 egg
1 tsp vanilla essence
50 g (2 oz) unsalted butter, melted
200 g (7 oz) chopped dates

for the topping
200 g (7 oz) brown sugar
50 g (2 oz) unsalted butter
500 ml (16½ fl oz) boiling water

Preheat the oven to 190°C (375°F / Gas mark 5). Line 8 muffin tins with greaseproof paper. In a medium bowl, combine the flour and sugar. In a separate medium bowl, beat the milk, egg, vanilla and butter until smooth and pale, about 2 to 3 minutes. Pour the batter over the flour mixture and stir with a wooden spoon. Fold in the dates. Scrape the mixture into the muffin tins, filling each cup about halfway. For the topping, sprinkle 1 tablespoon of the sugar on top of the batter in each cup. Put a half-tablespoon piece of butter on top of each cupcake, then pour about 1 tablespoon water over each.

Bake for 25 minutes. Remove from oven and cool for 5 minutes in the pan. Invert onto plates, peel off the greaseproof paper and serve immediately.

Makes 8

variations

florentine cupcakes

see base recipe page 117

chocolate chip florentine cupcakes
Prepare the basic cupcake recipe, adding 100 g (3½ oz) plain chocolate chips after creaming the batter.

cherry florentine cupcakes
Prepare the basic cupcake recipe, adding 3 tablespoons chopped glacé cherries after creaming the batter.

almond florentine cupcakes
Prepare the basic cupcake recipe, adding 3 tablespoons chopped blanched almonds after creaming the batter.

tipsy florentine cupcakes
Prepare the basic cupcake recipe, substituting 60 ml (2 fl oz) Amaretto for 60 ml (2 fl oz) of the buttermilk.

variations

strawberries & cream cupcakes

see base recipe page 118

strawberries & white chocolate cupcakes
Prepare the basic cupcake recipe, adding 100 g (3½ oz) white chocolate chips to the creamed batter.

strawberries & honey cupcakes
Prepare the basic cupcake recipe. For the topping, substitute 2 tablespoons honey for the icing sugar.

strawberries & lime cupcakes
Prepare the basic cupcake recipe. For the topping, substitute 1 tablespoon lime juice for the vanilla essence. Substitute 4 tablespoons lime marmalade for the strawberry jam.

berries & cream cupcakes
Prepare the basic cupcake recipe. For the topping, substitute 1 lb (450 g) mixed berries for the strawberries.

variations

baked cheesecakes

see base recipe page 120

banana & raisin baked cheesecakes
Prepare the basic cupcake recipe, adding 115 g (4 oz) mashed banana (about
1 banana) to the cheese mixture before adding the eggs. Add 4 tablespoons
raisins to the mixture after adding the egg.

raspberry baked cheesecakes
Prepare the basic cupcake recipe, adding 100 g (3½ oz) fresh raspberries after
mixing in the eggs.

maple syrup baked cheesecakes
Prepare the basic cupcake recipe, substituting 100 g (3½ oz) maple syrup for the
icing sugar.

almond baked cheesecakes
Prepare the basic cupcake recipe, substituting 1 teaspoon almond essence for
2 teaspoons vanilla.

kahlua & orange cupcakes

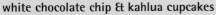

see base recipe page 122

white chocolate chip & kahlua cupcakes
Prepare the basic cupcake recipe, adding 100 g (3½ oz) white chocolate chips to the creamed batter.

plain chocolate chip & kahlua cupcakes
Prepare the basic cupcake recipe, adding 100 g (3½ oz) plain dark chocolate chips to the creamed batter.

raisin, brazil nut & kahlua cupcakes
Prepare the basic cupcake recipe, adding 50 g (2 oz) raisins and 50 g (2 oz) chopped Brazil nuts to the creamed batter

cointreau & orange cupcakes
Prepare the basic cupcake recipe, substituting Cointreau for Kahlua in the icing.

hot chocolate fondant cupcakes

see base recipe page 123

strawberry cream fondant cupcakes
Prepare the basic cupcake recipe. Purée 5 medium-sized fresh strawberries in a food processor. Beat 240 ml (8 oz) cream with 1 teaspoon vanilla essence until it is soft but holds its shape. Fold in the puréed strawberries. Spoon over the hot cupcakes. Omit the basic topping.

orange cream fondant cupcakes
Prepare the basic cupcake recipe. Beat 240 ml (8 oz) whipping cream with 1 teaspoon orange essence and 2 tablespoons icing sugar until it is soft but holds its shape. Spoon liberally over the hot cupcakes. Omit the basic topping.

crème chantilly fondant cupcakes
Prepare the basic cupcake recipe. Beat 240 ml (8 fl oz) whipping cream with 1 teaspoon vanilla essence and 2 tablespoons icing sugar until it is soft but holds its shape. Spoon over the hot cupcakes. Omit the basic topping.

cappuccino fondant cupcakes
Prepare the basic cupcake recipe, adding 1 teaspoon cinnamon to the batter. Beat 240 ml (8 fl oz) cream with 1 teaspoon coffee essence and 2 tablespoons icing sugar until it is soft but holds its shape. Spoon liberally over the hot cupcakes. Omit the basic topping.

variations

brioche bread pudding cupcakes

see base recipe page 125

blueberry bread pudding cupcakes
Prepare the basic cupcake recipe, substituting 100 g (3½ oz) fresh blueberries
for the raspberries.

cherry bread pudding cupcakes
Prepare the basic cupcake recipe, substituting 100 g (3½ oz) chopped glacé
cherries for the raspberries.

chocolate chip bread pudding cupcakes
Prepare the basic cupcake recipe, substituting 100 g (3½ oz) plain chocolate
chips for the raspberries.

berry delicious bread pudding cupcakes
Prepare the basic cupcake recipe, substituting 45 g (1½ oz) each of
raspberries, blueberries and sliced strawberries for the raspberries.

variations

mini espresso cupcakes

see base recipe page 126

mini chocolate espresso cupcakes
Prepare the basic cupcake recipe, adding 3 tablespoons chocolate chips after creaming the batter.

mini cinnamon espresso cupcakes
Prepare the basic cupcake recipe, sieving 2 teaspoons cinnamon into the dry ingredients.

mini espresso cupcakes with tia maria
Prepare the basic cupcake recipe, adding 2 tablespoons Tia Maria liqueur to the icing.

mini caramel macchiatto cupcakes
Prepare the basic cupcake recipe. When the cupcakes have cooled, use a sharp knife to slice off the tops. Using a teaspoon, hollow out a small hole in the top of each cupcake. Spoon 1 teaspoon prepared caramel sauce into the small hole. Place the top back on the cupcake and ice.

almond & raspberry friands

see base recipe page 129

strawberry friands
Prepare the basic cupcake recipe, substituting 100 g (3½ oz) fresh
strawberries for the raspberries.

chocolate & pecan friands
Prepare the basic cupcake recipe, substituting 3 tablespoons chopped pecans
and 3 tablespoons plain chocolate chips for the raspberries.

raisin friands
Prepare the basic cupcake recipe, substituting 100 g (3½ oz) raisins for
the raspberries.

almond & pear friands
Prepare the basic cupcake recipe, substituting 100 g (3½ oz) peeled and
chopped pears for the raspberries.

variations

lime meringue cupcakes

see base recipe page 131

ice cream meringue cupcakes
Prepare the basic cupcake recipe, substituting 1 teaspoon ice cream for the
original filling in each cupcake. Pop the cupcakes into the freezer until ready
to serve.

chocolate meringue cupcakes
Prepare the basic cupcake recipe. For the filling, substitute 100 g (3½ oz) plain
chocolate chips for the milk and lime juice. Melt the chocolate in a medium pan
over a pan of simmering water and cool slightly. Spoon the chocolate into the
hole and refrigerate until set. Decorate with the meringue when the chocolate
has cooled. Bake for 5 minutes until meringue is golden.

lemon meringue cupcakes
Prepare the basic cupcake recipe. For the filling, substitute 75 ml (3 fl oz) lemon
juice for the lime juice.

mango cupcakes
Prepare the basic cupcake recipe. For the filling, substitute 75 ml (3 fl oz) mango
nectar for the lime juice.

pineapple upside-down cupcakes

see base recipe page 132

cherry & pineapple upside-down cupcakes
Prepare the basic cupcake recipe. Add 100 g (3½ oz) chopped cherries to the
pineapple mixture.

almond & pineapple upside-down cupcakes
Prepare the basic cupcake recipe, adding 3 tablespoons chopped blanched
almonds to the cupcake batter.

orange & pineapple upside-down cupcakes
Prepare the basic cupcake recipe, adding 2 teaspoons orange essence to the
cupcake batter.

pineapple & coconut upside-down cupcakes
Prepare the basic cupcake recipe, adding 45 g (1½ oz) desiccated coconut to
the cupcake batter.

apple brandy upside-down cupcakes
Prepare the basic cupcake recipe. Replace the pineapple mixture with 570 g
(1 lb 4 oz) apples, peeled, cored and sliced, 115 g (4 oz) unsalted butter,
melted, 115 g (4 oz) brown sugar and 4 tablespoons apple brandy. Combine,
and proceed as main recipe.

variations

little caramel cupcakes

see base recipe page 134

chocolate chip & caramel cupcakes
Prepare the basic cupcake recipe, mixing 4 tablespoons plain chocolate chips into the batter after the milk has been added.

ginger & caramel cupcakes
Prepare the basic cupcake recipe, mixing 3 tablespoons chopped crystallised ginger into the batter after the milk has been added.

chocolate nougat cupcakes
Prepare the basic cupcake recipe, substituting 8 mini nougat bars for the caramel.

peanut butter cup cupcakes
Prepare the basic cupcake recipe, substituting 100 g (3½ oz) chopped chocolate-covered peanut butter cups for the caramel.

variations

sticky toffee pudding cupcakes

see base recipe page 135

date & apricot pudding cupcakes
Prepare the basic cupcake recipe. Substitute 200 g (7 oz) dried apricots for half the chopped dates.

date & walnut pudding cupcakes
Prepare the basic cupcake recipe. Substitute 200 g (7 oz) chopped walnuts for half the chopped dates.

date & pistachio pudding cupcakes
Prepare the basic cupcake recipe. Substitute 200 g (7 oz) chopped pistachios for half the chopped dates.

sticky figgy pudding cupcakes
Prepare the basic cupcake recipe. Substitute 115 g (4 oz) chopped dried figs for the chopped dates.

celebration cupcakes

This chapter will provide inspiration for your next

special occasion, whether a holiday like Valentine's

Day, or a birthday or wedding.

easter egg nests

see variations page 164

These cute nests make the perfect gift for your little Easter bunnies.

for the cupcakes
225 g (8 oz) unsalted butter, softened
225 g (8 oz) caster sugar
225 g (8 oz) self-raising flour
4 eggs
1 tsp vanilla essence

for the icing
275 g (10 oz) chocolate, flaked
2 tbsp double cream
100 g (3½ oz) plain chocolate, chopped
54 mini chocolate eggs

Preheat the oven to 175°C (350°F / Gas mark 4). Place 18 paper baking cases in muffin tins. Combine all the cupcake ingredients in a large bowl and beat with an electric whisk until smooth and pale, about 2 to 3 minutes. Spoon the batter into the cases. Bake for 20 minutes. Remove pans from the oven and cool for 5 minutes. Then remove the cupcakes and cool on a rack.

To make the icing, put the plain chocolate and cream in a small saucepan over a low heat. Stir gently until combined. Remove from the heat and stir until the mixture is smooth. Swirl onto the cooled cupcakes. Top with flaked chocolate and place 3 mini eggs on top of each one.

Store without icing in an airtight container for up to 3 days, or freeze for up to 3 months.

Makes 1½ dozen

wedding cupcakes

see variations page 165

These cupcakes are perfect for a home-style wedding. Each of your guests can take one home as a memento of the day.

for the cupcakes
225 g (8 oz) unsalted butter, softened
225 g (8 oz) caster sugar
225 g (8 oz) self-raising flour
4 eggs
1 tsp vanilla essence

for the icing
275 g (10 oz) icing sugar
2 tbsp lemon juice
54 sugared almonds
18 iced roses

Preheat the oven to 175°C (350°F / Gas mark 4). Place 18 paper baking cases in muffin tins. Combine all the cupcake ingredients in a large bowl and beat with an electric whisk until smooth and pale, about 2 to 3 minutes.

Spoon the batter into the cases. Bake for 20 minutes. Remove tins from the oven and cool for 5 minutes. Then remove the cupcakes and cool on a rack.

To make the icing, sieve the icing sugar into a medium bowl. Add the lemon juice gradually, until it holds its shape. Spread onto the cupcakes, and top with almonds and roses.

Store without icing in an airtight container for up to 3 days, or freeze for up to 3 months.

Makes 1½ dozen

passover cupcakes

see variations page 166

Make these with matzoh meal, also known as cake meal. We have added fresh blueberries to these passover treats.

225 g (8 oz) caster sugar
115 ml (4 fl oz) vegetable oil
3 eggs
60 g (2½ oz) matzoh meal

2 tbsp potato starch
1 tsp cinnamon
225 g (8 oz) blueberries

Preheat the oven to 175°C (350°F / Gas mark 4). Place 12 paper baking cases in a muffin tin.

In a medium bowl, beat the sugar, oil and eggs with an electric whisk for 2 to 3 minutes. Set aside. In a small bowl, sieve together the matzoh meal, potato starch and cinnamon. Add the dry ingredients to the egg mixture. Stir in the blueberries. Spoon the mixture into the cases.

Bake for 20 minutes. Remove pan from the oven and cool for 5 minutes. Then remove the cupcakes and cool on a rack.

Store in an airtight container for up to 3 days, or freeze for up to 3 months.

Makes 1 dozen

irish barm brack cupcakes

see variations page 167

Traditionally, a coin and a ring are hidden in barm brack cakes. The person who finds the ring will soon be married and the person who finds the coin will soon be wealthy.

100 g (3½ oz) raisins
100 g (3½ oz) sultanas
100 g (3½ oz) currants
225 ml (8 fl oz) brewed black tea
450 g (1 lb) plain flour
1 tsp mixed spice

75 g (3 oz) brown sugar
1 tsp baking powder
pinch of salt
1 egg
115 g (4 oz) unsalted butter, melted

In a large bowl, soak the dried fruits in the tea. Leave overnight or for a minimum of 6 hours.

Preheat the oven to 200°C (400°F / Gas mark 6). Grease a 12-cup muffin tin with a little oil.

Mix the dry ingredients in a large bowl. In a separate large bowl, mix the egg and butter. Add the soaked and strained fruit, and stir well. Fold in the flour mixture.

Spoon the mixture into the prepared tin. (Optional: Place a ring in one of the cakes, and a coin in another.) Bake until the cupcakes are a dark golden colour. Remove tin from the oven and cool for 5 minutes. Then remove the cupcakes and cool on a rack. Serve with unsalted butter.

Store in an airtight container for up to 5 days, or freeze for up to 3 months.

Makes 1 dozen

king cupcakes

see variations page 168

Our version of the classic Mardi Gras 'king cake'. The colours traditionally used on the cake represent justice, faith and power.

for the cupcakes
225 g (8 oz) unsalted butter, softened
225 g (8 oz) caster sugar
225 g (8 oz) self-raising flour
4 eggs
1 tsp vanilla essence

for the icing
275 g (10 oz) icing sugar
2 tbsp lemon juice
2 tbsp gold-coloured sugar crystals
2 tbsp green-coloured sugar crystals
2 tbsp purple-coloured sugar crystals

Preheat the oven to 175°C (350°F / Gas mark 4). Place 18 paper baking cases in muffin tins. Combine all the cupcake ingredients in a large bowl and beat with an electric whisk until smooth and pale, about 2 to 3 minutes. Spoon the batter into the cases. Bake for 20 minutes. Remove tins from the oven and cool for 5 minutes. Then remove the cupcakes and cool on a rack.

To make the icing, sieve the icing sugar in a medium bowl. Slowly add the lemon juice until the mixture becomes firm but spreadable. Spread onto the cupcakes, and sprinkle with the coloured sugar.

Store without icing in an airtight container for up to 3 days, or freeze for up to 3 months.

Makes 1½ dozen

christmas tree cupcakes

see variations page 169

These fun and festive little cakes will look superb on your Christmas dessert table. You can find ready-rolled fondant icing at cake decorating and baking supply shops.

for the cupcakes
225 g (8 oz) unsalted butter, softened
225 g (8 oz) caster sugar
225 g (8 oz) self-raising flour
4 eggs
1 tsp vanilla essence

for the icing
175 g (6 oz) ready-rolled white fondant icing
175 g (6 oz) ready-rolled green fondant icing
2 tbsp raspberry jam
coloured balls, to decorate

Preheat the oven to 175°C (350°F / Gas mark 4). Place 18 paper baking cases in muffin tins. Combine all the cupcake ingredients into a large bowl and beat with an electric whisk until smooth and pale, about 2 to 3 minutes. Spoon the batter into the cases. Bake for 20 minutes. Remove tins from the oven and cool for 5 minutes. Then remove the cupcakes and cool on a rack. Dust 2 baking sheets with icing sugar. To make the icing, roll the white fondant to 3 mm (⅛ in) thick. Cut 18 circles using a 6-cm (2½-in) biscuit cutter and set them on one of the baking sheets. Roll the green fondant to 3 mm (⅛ in) thick. Using a small Christmas tree biscuit cutter, cut shapes out of the icing and place them on the other baking sheet to firm a little. Brush each cupcake with a little raspberry jam, then place a white fondant disc on top. Top with a Christmas tree and decorate with the coloured balls.

Makes 1½ dozen

snowflake cupcakes

see variations page 170

These cupcakes are delightful for a Christmas gathering. You can serve them on
Christmas Eve when Santa's sleigh has set off and the kids are tucked into bed.

for the cupcakes
225 g (8 oz) unsalted butter, softened
225 g (8 oz) caster sugar
225 g (8 oz) self-raising flour
4 eggs
1 tsp vanilla essence

for the icing
115 g (4 oz) unsalted butter, softened
225 (8 oz) icing sugar, sieved
1 tsp vanilla essence
2 tsp pale dry sherry
4 tbsp desiccated coconut

Preheat the oven to 175°C (350°F / Gas mark 4). Place 18 paper baking cases in muffin tins.
Combine all the cupcake ingredients in a large bowl and beat with an electric whisk until
smooth and pale, about 2 to 3 minutes. Spoon the batter into the cases. Bake for 20 minutes.
Remove tins from the oven and cool for 5 minutes. Then remove the cupcakes and cool on
a rack.

For the icing, beat the butter, icing sugar, vanilla and sherry in a medium bowl until smooth
and creamy. Spread on top of the cupcakes. Sprinkle a little coconut on top to resemble
snowflakes.

Store without icing in an airtight container for up to 3 days, or freeze for up to 3 months.

Makes 1½ dozen

independence day cupcakes

see variations page 171

With their red, white and blue icing, these cupcakes make for a festive Fourth of July!

for the cupcakes
225 g (8 oz) unsalted butter, softened
225 g (8 oz) caster sugar
225 g (8 oz) self-raising flour
4 eggs
1 tsp vanilla essence

for the icing
115 g (4 oz) unsalted butter, softened
225 g (8 oz) icing sugar, sieved
1 tsp vanilla essence
200 g (7 oz) ready-rolled white fondant icing
175 g (6 oz) ready-rolled blue fondant icing
175 g (6 oz) ready-rolled red fondant icing

Preheat the oven to 175°C (350°F / Gas mark 4). Place 18 paper baking cases in muffin tins. Combine all the cupcake ingredients in a large bowl and beat with an electric whisk until smooth and pale, about 2 to 3 minutes. Spoon the batter into the cases. Bake for 20 minutes. Remove tins from the oven and cool for 5 minutes. Then remove the cupcakes and cool on a rack.

To make the icing, beat the butter and icing sugar until soft. Add the vanilla and beat again. Spread onto the cooled cupcakes. Roll white fondant to 3 mm (⅛ in) thick. Cut out 18 circles using a 6-cm (2½-in) biscuit cutter and lay on top of the frosted cupcakes. Roll out red and blue fondant to 3 mm (⅛ in) thick. Cut out stars and thin stripes of the colours and lay them on white fondant, mimicking the look of the American flag. Store without icing in an airtight container for up to 3 days.

Makes 1½ dozen

love-heart cupcakes

see variations page 172

These cupcakes make a delightful romantic gift for your true love on Valentine's Day – don't forget to attach a lover's message!

for the cupcakes
225 g (8 oz) unsalted butter, softened
225 g (8 oz) caster sugar
225 g (8 oz) self-raising flour
4 eggs
1 tsp vanilla essence

for the icing
175 g (6 oz) ready-rolled red fondant icing
175 g (6 oz) ready-rolled white fondant icing
3 tbsp raspberry jam
silver balls

Preheat the oven to 175°C (350°F / Gas mark 4). Dust two baking sheets with icing sugar and put aside. Place 18 paper baking cases in muffin tins. Combine all the cupcake ingredients in a large bowl and beat with an electric whisk until smooth and pale, about 2 to 3 minutes. Spoon the batter into the cases. Bake for 20 minutes. Remove tins from the oven and cool for 5 minutes. Then remove cupcakes and cool on a rack.

To make the icing, roll the white fondant icing to 3 mm (1/8 in) thick. Cut 18 circles using a 6-cm (2 1/2-in) biscuit cutter, and set them on one of the baking sheets. Roll the red fondant icing to 3 mm (1/8 in) thick. Using a heart-shaped cutter, cut out 18 small hearts and set them on the other baking sheet. Brush each cupcake with a little jam and lay a white circle on top. Place a heart on top of the circle. Decorate with silver balls around the edge. Store without icing in an airtight container for up to 3 days, or freeze for up to 3 months.

Makes 1 1/2 dozen

birthday cupcakes

see variations page 173

This is an easy and fun way to personalise birthday cupcakes!

for the cupcakes
225 g (8 oz) unsalted butter, softened
225 g (8 oz) caster sugar
225 g (8 oz) self-raising flour
4 eggs
1 tsp vanilla essence

for the icing
115 g (4 oz) unsalted butter, softened
225 g (8 oz) icing sugar, sieved
1 tsp vanilla essence
200 g (7 oz) ready-rolled white fondant icing
175 g (6 oz) ready-rolled blue fondant icing
175 g (6 oz) ready-rolled red fondant icing
silver balls

Preheat the oven to 175°C (350°F / Gas mark 4). Place 18 paper baking cases in muffin tins. Combine all the cupcake ingredients in a large bowl and beat with an electric whisk until smooth and pale, about 2 to 3 minutes. Spoon the batter into the cases. Bake for 20 minutes. Remove tins from the oven and cool for 5 minutes. Then remove the cupcakes and cool on a rack.

For the icing, beat the butter and icing sugar in a medium bowl until soft and creamy. Add the vanilla and beat again. Spread onto the cooled cupcakes. Roll the white fondant to 3 mm (⅛ in) thick. Cut 18 circles using a 6-cm (2½-in) biscuit cutter. Lay on top of the iced cupcakes. Roll the red and blue fondant to 3 mm (⅛ in) thick. Using mini alphabet biscuit cutters, cut out initials and decorate the cupcakes. Garnish with silver balls.

Makes 1½ dozen

variations

easter egg nests

see base recipe page 149

silver egg nests
Prepare the basic cupcake recipe, substituting 54 silver sugared almonds for the mini chocolate eggs.

orange-flavoured egg nests
Prepare the basic cupcake recipe, adding 1 teaspoon orange essence to the chocolate icing.

chocolate chip egg nests
Prepare the basic cupcake recipe, folding 100 g (3½ oz) plain chocolate chips into the batter.

easter egg baskets
Prepare the basic cupcake recipe. In place of chopped chocolate, use desiccated coconut coloured with green food colouring. Bend a pipe cleaner and attach to each cupcake as a basket handle.

jelly bean baskets
Prepare the basic cupcake recipe. In place of chopped chocolate, use desiccated coconut coloured with green food colouring. Subtitute jelly beans for mini chocolate eggs. Bend a pipe cleaner and attach to each cupcake as a basket handle.

variations

wedding cupcakes

see base recipe page 150

primrose wedding cupcakes
Prepare the basic cupcake recipe, substituting 18 iced primroses for
the roses.

chocolate wedding cupcakes
Prepare the basic cupcake recipe, folding 100 g (3½ oz) plain chocolate chips
into the creamed batter.

amaretto wedding cupcakes
Drizzle 3 tablespoons Amaretto over the cooled cupcakes before
icing them.

rose petal wedding cupcakes
Prepare the basic cupcake recipe, substituting 7 g (¼ oz) fresh, fragrant rose
petals for the iced roses and almonds.

elegant wedding cupcakes
Prepare the basic cupcake recipe, substituting 7 g (¼ oz) fresh, fragrant
white rose petals for the iced roses and almonds. Ice the cupcakes, sprinkle
with crystal sanding sugar, then top with rose petals.

variations

passover cupcakes

see base recipe page 152

cranberry passover cupcakes
Prepare the basic cupcake recipe, substituting 225 g (8 oz) fresh cranberries for the blueberries.

orange & raisin passover cupcakes
Prepare the basic cupcake recipe, substituting 100 g (3½ oz) raisins for the blueberries. Add 1 teaspoon orange essence to the egg mixture.

lemon & ginger passover cupcakes
Prepare the basic cupcake recipe, substituting 1 tablespoon lemon zest and 3 tablespoons chopped crystallised ginger for the blueberries.

cherry & almond passover cupcakes
Prepare the basic cupcake recipe, substituting almond essence for the cinnamon and 100 g (3½ oz) dried cherries for the blueberries.

date & almond passover cupcakes
Prepare the basic cupcake recipe, substituting almond essence for the cinnamon and 75 g (2½ oz) dried chopped dates for the blueberries.

variations

irish barm brack cupcakes

see base recipe page 153

sugar-glazed barm brack cupcakes
Prepare the basic cupcake recipe. Prepare a glaze by mixing 2 tablespoons
boiling water with 1 tablespoon caster sugar. Brush the glaze on the
cupcakes while they are still warm in the tin. Return the tin to the oven for
a few minutes to allow the glaze to set and turn a shiny brown.

whiskey-glazed barm brack cupcakes
Prepare the basic cupcake recipe. Prepare a glaze by mixing 2 tablespoons
warm Irish whiskey with 1 tablespoon caster sugar. Brush the glaze on the
cupcakes while they are still warm in the tin. Return the tin to the oven for
a few minutes to allow the glaze to set and turn a shiny brown.

apricot barm brack cupcakes
Prepare the basic cupcake recipe, adding 100 g (3½ oz) chopped
dried apricots to the dried fruit mixture. Increase quantity of black tea
to 300 ml (10 fl oz).

boston irish barm brack cupcakes
Prepare the basic cupcake recipe, adding 100 g (3½ oz) plain chocolate chips
after creaming.

variations

king cupcakes

see base recipe page 154

sultana king cupcakes
Prepare the basic cupcake recipe, folding 100 g (3½ oz) sultanas into the creamed batter.

walnut king cupcakes
Prepare the basic cupcake recipe, folding 100 g (3½ oz) chopped walnuts into the creamed batter.

white chocolate king cupcakes
Prepare the basic cupcake recipe, folding 100 g (3½ oz) white chocolate chips into the creamed batter.

baby shower cupcakes
Prepare the basic cupcake recipe. For the decoration, substitute pastel yellow, blue, green and pink sugars in place of gold, green and purple.

christmas tree cupcakes

see base recipe page 156

ginger & raisin christmas tree cupcakes
Prepare the basic cupcake recipe, adding 2 teaspoons ground ginger to the cupcake ingredients, and folding 100 g (3½ oz) raisins into the creamed batter.

orange & lemon christmas tree cupcakes
Prepare the basic cupcake recipe, adding 1 tablespoon grated orange zest and 1 tablespoon grated lemon zest to the creamed batter.

white chocolate christmas tree cupcakes
Prepare the basic cupcake recipe, folding 100 g (3½ oz) white chocolate chips into the creamed batter.

christmas ornament cupcakes
Prepare the basic cupcake recipe. Substitute cut-out circles, stars and stripes for Christmas trees and decorate the cupcakes.

easy christmas tree cupcakes
Prepare the basic recipe. For the decoration, substitute ready-made sugar paste Christmas trees or tiny Christmas tree biscuits for the coloured fondant.

variations

snowflake cupcakes

see base recipe page 158

poppy seed snowflake cupcakes
Prepare the basic cupcake recipe, adding 2 tablespoons poppy seeds to the creamed batter.

mixed berry snowflake cupcakes
Prepare the basic cupcake recipe, folding 4 tablespoons dried mixed cranberries, cherries and blueberries into the creamed batter.

hazelnut snowflake cupcakes
Prepare the basic cupcake recipe, folding 3 tablespoons roasted chopped hazelnuts into the creamed batter.

sparkly snowflake cupcakes
Prepare the basic cupcake recipe, sprinkling each cupcake with sparkly sanding sugar.

let-it-snow cupcakes
Prepare the basic cupcake recipe, sprinkling each cupcake with pearl sugar.

variations

independence day cupcakes

see base recipe page 159

raisin independence day cupcakes
Prepare the basic cupcake recipe, folding 100 g (3½ oz) raisins into the creamed batter.

white chocolate independence day cupcakes
Prepare the basic cupcake recipe, folding 100 g (3½ oz) white chocolate chips into the creamed batter.

crystallised peel independence day cupcakes
Prepare the basic cupcake recipe, folding 2 tablespoons chopped crystallised peel into the creamed batter.

red, white & blueberry independence day cupcakes
Prepare the basic cupcake recipe. For the icing, substitute prepared white icing for the fondant. Decorate the cupcakes with 115 g (4 oz) sliced strawberries and 125 g (4½ oz) whole blueberries.

sparkler cupcakes
Prepare the basic cupcake recipe. For the icing, substitute prepared white icing for the fondant. Decorate the cupcakes with sanding sugar and place a sparkler in the centre of each.

variations

love-heart cupcakes

see base recipe page 161

white chocolate heart cupcakes
Prepare the basic cupcake recipe, folding 100 g (3½ oz) white chocolate chips into the creamed batter.

macadamia nut heart cupcakes
Prepare the basic cupcake recipe, folding 100 g (3½ oz) lightly toasted and chopped macadamia nuts into the creamed batter.

cherry heart cupcakes
Prepare the basic cupcake recipe, folding 4 tablespoons chopped glacé cherries into the creamed batter.

raspberry heart cupcakes
Prepare the basic cupcake recipe, substituting prepared white icing for fondant. Decorate with 200 g (7 oz) fresh raspberries.

be mine heart cupcakes
Prepare the basic cupcake recipe, substituting prepared white icing for fondant. Decorate with 200 g (7 oz) valentine-themed heart sweets.

variations

birthday cupcakes

see base recipe page 162

cherry & almond birthday cupcakes
Prepare the basic cupcake recipe, folding 2 tablespoons chopped
crystallised cherries and 2 tablespoons chopped blanched almonds into
the creamed batter.

orange birthday cupcakes
Prepare the basic cupcake recipe, adding 1 teaspoon orange essence to the
creamed batter.

crystallised fruit birthday cupcakes
Prepare the basic cupcake recipe, folding 3 tablespoons chopped crystallised
citrus fruits into the creamed batter.

happy birthday cupcakes
Prepare the basic cupcake recipe, substituting prepared white icing for
fondant. Decorate with coloured sprinkles and place a small candle in the
centre of each cupcake.

cupcakes for kids

Crisp rice cupcakes and mini peanut butter cupcakes

are a great way to get kids involved in the kitchen.

These cupcakes are so much fun to decorate, it can

be a party in itself!

s'more cupcakes

see variations page 195

Building s'more cupcakes is great fun for everyone. They require little fuss and effort, with a quick assembly and baking time.

24 digestive biscuits
200 g (7 oz) plain chocolate bars, broken into
    12 squares
100 g (3¹/₂ oz) chopped walnuts

3 tbsp desiccated coconut
60 g (2¹/₂ oz) mini marshmallows

Preheat the oven to 160°C (325°C / Gas mark 3). Place 12 paper baking cases in a muffin tin. Lay a biscuit in the bottom of each case. Add a piece of chocolate, followed by a sprinkle of walnuts and coconut. Lay another biscuit on top.

Bake for 7 minutes, until the chocolate has melted. Remove tin from the oven. Push the biscuit 'lids' down so that they are secure.

Pop a couple of marshmallows on top of each cupcake. Return tin to the oven for 10 minutes, until the marshmallows melt and brown slightly.

Remove tin from the oven and cool for 5 minutes. Remove the cupcakes and cool on a rack.

Store in an airtight container for up to 24 hours.

Makes 1 dozen

toadstool cupcakes

see variations page 196

These funky toadstool cupcakes will brighten up any children's party. You can find white fondant icing and sugar paste cartoon characters at cake decorating and baking supply shops.

for the cupcakes
225 g (8 oz) unsalted butter, softened
225 g (8 oz) caster sugar
225 g (8 oz) self-raising flour
4 eggs
1 tsp vanilla essence

for the icing
375 g (13 oz) icing sugar, sieved
225 g (8 oz) unsalted butter, softened
pinch of salt
red food colouring
50 g (2 oz) ready-rolled white fondant icing

Preheat the oven to 175°C (350°F / Gas mark 4). Place 18 paper baking cases in muffin tins. Combine all the cupcake ingredients in a large bowl and beat with an electric whisk until smooth and pale, about 2 to 3 minutes. Spoon the batter into the cases. Bake for 20 minutes. Remove tins from the oven and cool for 5 minutes. Then remove the cupcakes and cool on a rack.

To make the icing, cream the icing sugar, butter and salt in a medium bowl with an electric whisk until smooth. Add a few drops of the food colouring, and mix until the icing is a uniform bright red. Cut small circles out of the fondant icing. Spoon the red icing onto the cupcakes and place the white fondant circles on top. Store without icing in an airtight container for up to 3 days, or freeze for up to 3 months.

Makes 1¹/₂ dozen

ice cream cone cupcakes

see variations page 197

These cupcakes look like ice cream – but they won't melt!

for the cupcakes
225 g (8 oz) unsalted butter, softened
225 g (8 oz) caster sugar
225 g (8 oz) self-raising flour
2 tsp baking powder
4 eggs
115 ml (4 fl oz) buttermilk
1 tsp vanilla essence
24 mini flat-bottomed wafer cups

for the icing
175 g (6 oz) icing sugar, sieved
115 g (4 oz) unsalted butter, softened
pinch of salt
115 ml (4 fl oz) cream
1 tsp vanilla essence
2 tbsp coloured sprinkles

Preheat the oven to 175°C (350°F / Gas mark 4). Line a 24-cup mini muffin tin with paper baking cases. Combine all the cupcake ingredients in a large bowl and beat with an electric whisk until smooth and pale, about 2 to 3 minutes. Spoon the batter into the cases. Bake for 20 minutes. Remove tin from the oven and cool for 5 minutes. Then remove the cupcakes and cool on a rack. Peel off the paper baking cases, and place the cupcakes inside the ice cream cones.

To make the icing, beat the icing sugar, butter and salt using an electric whisk. Add the cream and vanilla, and beat until smooth. Pipe the mixture in a swirl on top of the cupcake. Shake some sprinkles on top.

Store without icing in an airtight container for up to 2 days.

Makes 2 dozen

think pink cupcakes

see variations page 198

Think pink while you're icing and you will have a whole manner of coloured cupcakes!

for the cupcakes
225 g (8 oz) unsalted butter, softened
225 g (8 oz) caster sugar
225 g (8 oz) self-raising flour
2 tsp baking powder
4 eggs
1 tsp vanilla essence

for the icing
375 g (13 oz) icing sugar, sieved
225 g (8 oz) unsalted butter, softened
pinch of salt
pink food colouring
silver balls

Preheat the oven to 175°C (350°F / Gas mark 4). Place 18 paper baking cases in muffin tins. Combine all the cupcake ingredients in a large bowl and beat with an electric whisk until smooth and pale, about 2 to 3 minutes.

Spoon the batter into the cases. Bake for 20 minutes. Remove tins from the oven and cool for 5 minutes. Then remove the cupcakes and cool on a rack.

To make the icing, cream the icing sugar, butter and salt with an electric whisk until smooth. Add a few drops of food colouring, and mix well. Spread the icing liberally onto the cooled cupcakes and sprinkle with silver balls.

Store without icing in an airtight container for up to 3 days, or freeze for up to 3 months.

Makes 1½ dozen

cookies & cream cupcakes

see variations page 199

Mix crushed cookies into the batter to give a crispy crunch to these cupcakes.

for the cupcakes
225 g (8 oz) unsalted butter, softened
225 g (8 oz) caster sugar
225 g (8 oz) self-raising flour
2 tsp baking powder
4 eggs
1 tsp vanilla essence
10 crushed cream-filled chocolate cookies

for the icing
375 g (13 oz) icing sugar, sieved
225 g (8 oz) unsalted butter, softened
pinch of salt
10 chopped cream-filled chocolate cookies

Preheat the oven to 175°C (350°F / Gas mark 4). Place 18 foil or paper baking cases in muffin tins. Combine all the cupcake ingredients, except the cookies, in a large bowl and beat with an electric whisk until smooth and pale, about 2 to 3 minutes. Stir in the cookies.

Spoon the batter into the cases. Bake for 20 minutes. Remove tins from the oven and cool for 5 minutes. Then remove the cupcakes and cool on a wire rack.

To make the icing, beat the icing sugar, butter and salt using an electric whisk. Spread the icing onto the cooled cupcakes and sprinkle the chopped cookies on top.

Store without icing in an airtight container for up to 3 days, or freeze for up to 3 months.

Makes 1¹/₂ dozen

alphabet cupcakes

see variations page 200

Line these up to spell somebody's name at a birthday party! You can find ready-rolled fondant at cake decorator's or cake supply shops. Or use alphabet letter sweets.

for the cupcakes
225 g (8 oz) unsalted butter, softened
225 g (8 oz) caster sugar
225 g (8 oz) self-raising flour
2 tsp baking powder
4 eggs
1 tsp vanilla essence

for the icing
340 g (12 oz) ready-rolled white fondant icing
3 tbsp raspberry jam
50 g (2 oz) ready-rolled red fondant icing
50 g (2 oz) ready-rolled green fondant icing
50 g (2 oz) ready-rolled black fondant icing
coloured sprinkles

Preheat the oven to 350°F (175°C). Place 18 paper baking cases in muffin tins. Combine all the cupcake ingredients in a large bowl and beat with an electric whisk until smooth and pale, about 2 to 3 minutes. Spoon the batter into the cases. Bake for 20 minutes. Remove tins from the oven and cool for 5 minutes. Then remove the cupcakes and cool on a rack.

For the icing, roll out the white fondant and cut 18 circles using a 5-cm (2-in) biscuit cutter. Brush the cupcakes with a little of the jam. Press the circles onto the cupcakes. Roll out the remaining coloured fondant. Using mini alphabet cutters, cut letter shapes from the coloured fondant icing and place them on top of the white circles. Sprinkle the edges with coloured sprinkles.

Makes 1½ dozen

pineapple cupcakes

see variations page 201

These cupcakes melt in the mouth and are the perfect teatime treat.

for the cupcakes
225 g (8 oz) unsalted butter, softened
225 g (8 oz) caster sugar
225 g (8 oz) self-raising flour
1 tsp baking powder
4 eggs
1 tsp vanilla essence
175 g (6 oz) drained crushed pineapple

for the icing
200 g (7 oz) cream cheese, softened
175 g (6 oz) icing sugar, sieved
1 tbsp lemon juice
1 tsp vanilla essence
50 g (2 oz) chopped walnuts

Preheat the oven to 175°C (350°F / Gas mark 4). Place 18 paper baking cases in muffin tins. Combine all the cupcake ingredients, except the pineapple, in a large bowl and beat with an electric whisk for about 2 to 3 minutes. Stir in the pineapple. Spoon the batter into the cases. Bake for 20 minutes. Remove tins from the oven and cool for 5 minutes. Then remove the cupcakes and cool on a rack. To make the icing, slowly beat the cream cheese and icing sugar in a large bowl with an electric whisk until creamy and soft. Add the lemon juice and vanilla, and beat briskly until well combined. Spread the icing onto the cooled cupcakes and garnish with the chopped walnuts.

Store without icing in an airtight container for 2 to 3 days, or freeze for up to 3 months.

Makes 1 ½ dozen

mini peanut butter cupcakes

see variations page 202

Simple and no fuss. You can make these cupcakes in large batches, which makes them ideal for kids' parties and picnics.

375 g (13 oz) milk chocolate chips
30 g (1 oz) unsalted butter
3 tbsp double cream
175 g (6 oz) smooth peanut butter
12 peanut halves, to decorate

Place 12 mini foil baking cases in a muffin tin.

Place the chocolate, butter and cream in a medium bowl over a pan of simmering water, and stir until smooth. Remove from the heat and set aside.

With damp hands, shape the peanut butter into 12 small flat circles. Push the peanut butter into the bottom of the cases.

Pour the melted chocolate over the peanut butter, top each with a peanut half and refrigerate for at least 2 hours.

Store in an airtight container for up to 3 days.

Makes 1 dozen

crisp rice cupcakes

see variations page 203

I'm not too sure how many will reach the table, but these simple no-bake cupcakes are great fun for the budding young chef to try.

200 g (7 oz) dark chocolate
100 g (2½ oz) unsalted butter, softened
5 tbsp golden syrup
100 g (3½ oz) crisp rice cereal

Place 12 foil or paper baking cases on a tray.

Place the chocolate and butter in a medium bowl over a pan of simmering water, and stir until melted.

Remove tin from the heat and stir in the golden syrup and cereal. Drop spoonfuls of the mixture into the cases.

Refrigerate for 1 hour before serving.

Store in an airtight container for up to 5 days.

Makes 1 dozen

eggy cupcakes

see variations page 204

Don't worry – you won't have to crack whole eggs to get this lovely sunny-side-up look.
Serve these cupcakes for breakfast with a glass of freshly squeezed juice.

for the cupcakes
225 g (8 oz) unsalted butter, softened
225 g (8 oz) caster sugar
225 g (8 oz) self-raising flour
2 tsp baking powder
4 eggs
1 tsp vanilla essence

for the icing
375 g (13 oz) icing sugar, sieved
225 g (8 oz) unsalted butter, softened
pinch of salt
18 drained tinned peach halves

Preheat the oven to 175°C (350°F / Gas mark 4). Place 18 paper baking cases in muffin tins.
Combine all the cupcake ingredients in a large bowl and beat with an electric whisk until
smooth and pale, about 2 to 3 minutes. Spoon the batter into the cases. Bake for 20 minutes.
Remove tins from the oven and cool for 5 minutes. Then remove the cupcakes and cool on
a rack.

To make the icing, put the icing sugar, butter and salt in a large bowl and beat with an
electric whisk until smooth. Liberally spread the icing onto the cooled cupcakes and garnish
each cupcake with a peach half.

Store without icing in an airtight container for up to 3 days, or freeze for up to 3 months.

Makes 1¹/₂ dozen

chocolate berry cupcakes

see variations page 205

My good friend Beverley Glock gave me this recipe. She runs a company called 'Splat', which organises children's parties where both children and adults can bake.

for the cupcakes
100 g (3½ oz) fresh or thawed frozen
    blackberries
3 tbsp water
225 g (8 oz) caster sugar
100 g (3½ oz) self-raising flour
1 tsp baking powder
100 g (3½ oz) soft margarine

2 eggs
1 tbsp Dutch-process cocoa powder

for the ganache
150 g (5 oz) plain dark chocolate, broken
150 g (5 oz) cream
12 blackberries

Preheat the oven to 175°C (350°F / Gas mark 4). Place 12 mini paper baking cases in a muffin tin. Combine the blackberries, water and 115 g (4 oz) sugar in a small saucepan over low heat. Simmer for about 5 minutes, until the fruit starts to release its juices. Set aside to cool. Combine the rest of the ingredients in a medium bowl and beat with an electric whisk until pale and creamy, about 2 to 3 minutes. Spoon the batter into the cases. Spoon a little of the fruit on top. Bake for 20 minutes. Remove the tin and cool for 5 minutes. Then remove the cupcakes and cool on a rack. Store in an airtight container for up to 2 days, or freeze for up to 3 months. To make the ganache before serving, melt the chocolate and cream in a medium bowl over a pan of simmering water, until glossy and smooth. Dollop a spoonful of ganache onto each cooled cupcake and top with a blackberry. Refrigerate until set, then serve.

Store without ganache in an airtight container for up to 2 days, or freeze for up to 3 months.

Makes 1 dozen small cupcakes

space dust cupcakes

see variations page 206

Try these for a kids' party and watch their faces as the Space Dust explodes!

for the cupcakes
225 g (8 oz) unsalted butter, softened
225 g (8 oz) caster sugar
225 g (8 oz) self-raising flour
2 tsp baking powder
4 eggs
1 tsp vanilla essence

for the icing
115 g (4 oz) unsalted butter, softened
225 g (8 oz) icing sugar, sieved
1 tsp vanilla essence
2 sachets fruit-flavoured Space Dust

Preheat the oven to 175°C (350°F / Gas mark 4). Place 18 paper baking cases in muffin tins. Combine all cupcake ingredients in a large bowl and beat with an electric whisk until smooth and pale, about 2 to 3 minutes. Spoon the batter into the cases. Bake for 20 minutes.

Remove tins from the oven and cool for 5 minutes. Then remove the cupcakes and cool on a rack.

To make the icing, cream the butter, icing sugar and vanilla in a medium bowl until smooth. Smear onto the cupcakes and sprinkle with Space Dust.

Store without icing in an airtight container for up to 2 days, or freeze for up to 3 months.

Makes 1½ dozen

jam doughnut cupcakes

see variations page 207

These cupcakes aren't doughnuts, but I'm sure you'll see the likeness when you try one.

for the cupcakes
225 g (8 oz) unsalted butter, softened
225 g (8 oz) caster sugar
225 g (8 oz) self-raising flour
1 tsp baking powder
4 eggs
1 tsp vanilla essence
150 g (5 oz) raspberry jam

for the icing
200 g (7 oz) cream cheese, softened
175 g (6 oz) icing sugar, sieved
1 tbsp lemon juice
1 tsp vanilla essence

Preheat the oven to 175°C (350°F / Gas mark 4). Place 18 paper baking cases in muffin tins. Combine all the cupcake ingredients, except the jam, in a large bowl and beat with an electric whisk, about 2 to 3 minutes. Spoon the batter into the cases. Bake for 20 minutes.

Remove tins from the oven and cool for 5 minutes. Then remove the cupcakes and cool on a rack. Slice the top off each cupcake, hollow out a small hole with a teaspoon and fill with the jam. Replace the top. To make the icing, slowly beat the cream cheese and icing sugar in a large bowl with an electric whisk until creamy and soft. Add the lemon juice and vanilla, and beat briskly until well combined. Spread the icing onto the cupcakes.

Store without icing in an airtight container for up to 2 days, or freeze for up to 3 months.

Makes 1 ½ dozen

s'more cupcakes

see base recipe page 175

pecan s'more cupcakes
Prepare the basic cupcake recipe, substituting 100 g (3½ oz) roughly chopped pecans for the walnuts.

white chocolate s'more cupcakes
Prepare the basic cupcake recipe, substituting 50 g (2 oz) white chocolate chips for half the plain chocolate.

chocolate & raspberry s'more cupcakes
Prepare the basic cupcake recipe. Add 100 g (3 ½ oz) lightly crushed raspberries along with the coconut and walnuts.

banana s'more cupcakes
Prepare the basic cupcake recipe, substituting 1 fresh sliced banana for the walnuts.

strawberry s'more cupcakes
Prepare the basic cupcake recipe, substituting 115 g (4 oz) fresh sliced strawberries for the walnuts.

variations

toadstool cupcakes

see base recipe page 177

koala bear cupcakes
Prepare the basic cupcake recipe. Omit the rolled fondant. Colour the icing
with brown food colouring instead of red. Make a koala face on each
cupcake: A chocolate-covered Brazil nut for the nose, 2 walnut halves for
ears and 2 sweets for the eyes.

sneaky snake cupcakes
Prepare the basic cupcake recipe. For the icing, substitute 50 g (2 oz) green
ready-rolled fondant icing for the white fondant. Brush each cupcake with a
little fruit jam. Roll the green fondant thinly and, using a cookie cutter, cut
18 circles 6 cm (2½ in) across and place one on each cupcake. For the trees,
cut 6 chocolate sticks into 3 sections 5 cm (2 in) in length, and stand
upright on the fondant icing. Roll 50 g (2 oz) red fondant icing into
18 sausages 15 cm (6 in) in length. Curl the fondant around the chocolate
'trees' and decorate with 2 sweets for the eyes.

bling cupcakes
Prepare the basic cupcake recipe. Omit the rolled fondant. Decorate the red
icing on the cupcakes with silver and gold balls.

variations

ice cream cone cupcakes

see base recipe page 178

chocolate-iced cone cupcakes
Prepare the basic cupcake recipe. For the icing, add 100 g (3½ oz) chocolate chips along with the cream and vanilla.

choc & mint-iced cone cupcakes
Prepare the basic cupcake recipe. For the icing, add 100 g (3½ oz) mint chocolate chips along with the cream. Substitute 1 teaspoon mint essence for the vanilla.

honey & cream-iced cone cupcakes
Prepare the basic cupcake recipe. For the icing, add 75 g (3 oz) honey after creaming the icing sugar and butter.

strawberry ice cream cone cupcakes
Prepare the basic cupcake recipe. For the icing, substitute 50 g (2 oz) mashed fresh strawberries for the cream. Decorate with a strawberry on top of each cone.

caramel apple ice cream cone cupcakes
Prepare the basic cupcake recipe. For the icing, substitute 115 ml (4 fl oz) apple juice for the cream. Drizzle each cone with prepared caramel ice cream sauce.

variations

think pink cupcakes

see base recipe page 181

azure cupcakes
Prepare the basic cupcake recipe. For the icing, substitute blue food colouring for pink, and top with blue azure sugar crystals.

lavender sugar cupcakes
Prepare the basic cupcake recipe. For the icing, substitute blue food colouring for pink. Make lavender sugar by combining 3 tablespoons lavender flowers and 175 g (6 oz) caster sugar in a food processor for about 2 minutes. Put the sugar in a cool dry place, and let the flavours mingle for about 2 hours. Sprinkle on top of the icing.

rose sugar cupcakes
Prepare the basic cupcake recipe. Make rose-petal sugar by combining 3 tablespoons red rose petals and 175 g (6 oz) caster sugar in a food processor for about 2 minutes. Put the sugar in a cool dry place, and let the flavours mingle for about 2 hours. Sprinkle on top of the icing.

pink lemonade cupcakes
Prepare the basic cupcake recipe. For the icing, add 1 tablespoon sugar-free pink lemonade drink mix.

variations

cookies & cream cupcakes

see base recipe page 182

minted cookies & cream cupcakes
Prepare the basic cupcake recipe, using cream-filled mint chocolate cookies in both the cupcakes and the icing.

digestive biscuits & cream cupcakes
Prepare the basic cupcake recipe, substituting 100 g (3½ oz) crushed digestive biscuits for 10 cookies in the cupcakes, and another 100 g (3½ oz) crushed digestive biscuits for the cookies in the icing.

chocolate, nougat & cream cupcakes
Prepare the basic cupcake recipe, substituting 100 g (3½ oz) chopped chocolate nougat bars for 10 cookies in the cupcakes, and another 100 g (3½ oz) chopped nougat bars for the cookies in the icing.

peanut butter cookies & cream cupcakes
Prepare the basic cupcake recipe, using peanut butter cookies in both the cupcakes and the icing. Substitute 100 g (3½ oz) creamy peanut butter for half the butter in the icing.

variations

alphabet cupcakes

see base recipe page 184

white chocolate alphabet cupcakes
Prepare the basic cupcake recipe, adding 100 g (3½ oz) white chocolate chips to the creamed batter.

raisin alphabet cupcakes
Prepare the basic cupcake recipe, adding 100 g (3½ oz) raisins to the creamed batter.

number cupcakes
Prepare the basic cupcake recipe. Use mini number biscuit cutters instead of alphabet cutters.

easy alphabet cupcakes
Prepare the basic cupcake recipe. For the icing, substitute prepared white icing. Decorate with alphabet letter sweets.

big number cupcakes
Prepare the basic cupcake recipe. For the icing, substitute prepared white icing. On greaseproof paper, trace a circle the circumference of the cupcake top. Trace and cut out a number in the centre of the paper. Place the stencil on top of the iced cupcake and sprinkle coloured sugar to create the number.

variations

pineapple cupcakes

see base recipe page 185

kicked-up chilli pineapple cupcakes
Prepare the basic cupcake recipe. Add 1 teaspoon seeded and finely chopped chilli pepper to the creamed batter.

orange & pineapple cupcakes
Prepare the basic cupcake recipe. Add 2 tablespoons orange zest to the creamed batter.

coconut & pineapple cupcakes
Prepare the basic cupcake recipe. Add 65 g (2½ oz) desiccated coconut to the mixture after it has been creamed.

pineapple & marshmallow cupcakes
Prepare the basic cupcake recipe. Add 30 g (1 oz) coloured miniature marshmallows to the mixture after it has been creamed.

pineapple & chocolate chip cupcakes
Prepare the basic cupcake recipe. Add 75 g (3 oz) chocolate chips to the mixture after it has been creamed.

variations

mini peanut butter cupcakes

see base recipe page 186

mini marshmallow & peanut butter cupcakes
Prepare the basic cupcake recipe. Add 115 g (4 oz) chopped large
marshmallows to the melted chocolate mixture.

mini coconut & peanut butter cupcakes
Prepare the basic cupcake recipe. Add 3 tablespoons desiccated coconut to
the melted chocolate.

mini jam & peanut butter cupcakes
Prepare the basic cupcake recipe. Place a teaspoon of your favourite fruit
jam into the bottom of the baking cases and top with the peanut butter
and then the chocolate.

marshmallow & peanut butter cupcakes
Prepare the basic cupcake recipe. Place 2 miniature marshmallows into the
bottom of the baking cases and top with the peanut butter and then
the chocolate.

crisp rice cupcakes

see base recipe page 189

marshmallow & crisp rice cupcakes
Prepare the basic cupcake recipe. Stir in 25 g (1 oz) mini marshmallows along with the cereal.

raisins & crisp rice cupcakes
Prepare the basic cupcake recipe. Stir in 100 g (3½ oz) raisins along with the cereal.

cherry & crisp rice cupcakes
Prepare the basic cupcake recipe. Stir in 100 g (3½ oz) chopped red glacé cherries along with the cereal.

bird's nest cupcakes
Prepare the basic cupcake recipe. Drop spoonfuls of the mixture into the cases, then make a nest shape with the spoon. Fill each nest with tiny coloured sugar balls.

variations

eggy cupcakes

see base recipe page 190

kiwi cupcakes
Prepare the basic cupcake recipe, substituting 18 thin slices kiwi fruit for the peach halves.

nectarine cupcakes
Prepare the basic cupcake recipe, substituting 18 nectarine halves for the peach halves.

custard (runny egg) cupcakes
Prepare the basic cupcake recipe. Slice a thin circle off the top of each cooled cupcake. Using a teaspoon, make a small hole about 2½ cm (1 in) deep. Pipe 1 teaspoon prepared custard into the hole. Replace the 'lid', ice and add the peach half.

hit-the-target cupcakes
Prepare the basic cupcake recipe. On greaseproof paper, trace a circle the circumference of the cupcake top. Trace and cut out a circle in the centre of the paper. Place the stencil on top of the iced cupcake and sprinkle coloured sugar to create the bull's-eye.

chocolate berry cupcakes

see base recipe page 192

chocolate–raspberry cupcakes
Prepare the basic cupcake recipe, substituting 100 g (3½ oz) fresh raspberries for the blackberries.

chocolate–blueberry cupcakes
Prepare the basic cupcake recipe, substituting 100 g (3½ oz) fresh blueberries for the blackberries.

chocolate–cherry cupcakes
Prepare the basic cupcake recipe, substituting 100 g (3½ oz) fresh cherries for the blackberries.

chocolate–strawberry cupcakes
Prepare the basic cupcake recipe, substituting 100 g (3½ oz) fresh strawberries for the blackberries.

variations

space dust cupcakes

see base recipe page 193

ginger space dust cupcakes
Prepare the basic cupcake recipe, adding 1 teaspoon ground ginger and
3 tablespoons crystallised ginger to the creamed cupcake batter.

cherry space dust cupcakes
Prepare the basic cupcake recipe, adding 100 g (3½ oz) chopped crystallised
cherries to the creamed cupcake batter.

pineapple space dust cupcakes
Prepare the basic cupcake recipe, adding 100 g (3½ oz) chopped dried
pineapple to the creamed cupcake batter.

strawberry surprise space dust cupcakes
Prepare the basic cupcake recipe, dropping 1 teaspoon of strawberry jam
in the centre of each cupcake before baking. Use strawberry Space Dust on
the icing.

jam doughnut cupcakes

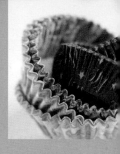

see base recipe page 194

boston cream doughnut cupcakes
Prepare the basic cupcake recipe. Substitute 115 ml (4 fl oz) vanilla custard
for the raspberry jam.

chocolate custard doughnut cupcakes
Prepare the basic cupcake recipe. Substitute 115 ml (4 fl oz) chocolate
custard for the raspberry jam.

marmalade doughnut cupcakes
Prepare the basic cupcake recipe. Substitute 150 g (5 oz) orange marmalade
for the raspberry jam.

peanut butter & jam doughnut cupcakes
Prepare the basic cupcake recipe. For the icing, substitute creamy peanut
butter for the cream cheese.

cupcakes for special diets

Moist and sweet banana and honey cupcakes, dairy-free berry cupcakes, gluten-free pecan cupcakes and chocolate vegan cupcakes – anyone with special dietary requirements will be well catered for with the selection of recipes in this chapter.

mini couscous cupcakes

see variations page 234

Couscous, the world's smallest pasta, is a staple throughout northern Africa. It gives these cupcakes a light and elegant texture.

100 g (3½ oz) couscous
115 ml (4 fl oz) boiling water
225 g (8 oz) plain flour
2 tbsp caster sugar
1 tbsp baking powder
pinch of salt
1 tsp cumin seeds, toasted

1 tsp ground coriander
1 egg
4 tbsp olive oil
1 tbsp lemon zest
2 tbsp chopped flat-leaf parsley

Preheat the oven to 175°C (350°F / Gas mark 4). Place 24 mini paper cases in a muffin tin. Put the couscous in a medium bowl and pour the boiling water over it. Cover and leave for 5 minutes, so the grains absorb the liquid. Fluff the grains apart with a fork.

Mix the dry ingredients in a bowl with a spoon. Beat the egg and oil in a large bowl with an electric whisk until combined. Add the couscous and the dry ingredients and mix until nearly combined. Fold in the lemon zest and parsley. Spoon the mixture into the cases. Bake for 20 minutes. Remove tin from the oven and cool for 5 minutes. Then remove the cupcakes and cool on a rack.

Store in an airtight container for up to 3 days, or freeze for up to 3 months.

Makes 2 dozen mini cakes

basil pesto cupcakes

see variations page 235

These unusually savoury cupcakes make an ideal wholesome treat.

for the cupcakes
115 g (4 oz) yellow polenta
115 g (4 oz) plain flour
2 tsp baking powder
3 tbsp sugar
pinch of salt
2 eggs

240 ml (8 fl oz) whole milk
50 g (2 oz) unsalted butter, melted

for the icing
115 g (4 oz) basil pesto
350 g (12 oz) cream cheese, softened
12 cherry tomatoes

Preheat the oven to 175°C (350°F / Gas mark 4). Place 12 paper baking cases into a muffin tin. In a medium bowl, stir the dry ingredients. Beat the eggs, milk and butter in a large bowl with an electric whisk until combined. Add the flour mixture to the egg mixture, and stir until just combined. Spoon the batter into the cases. Bake for 20 minutes. Remove tin and cool for 5 minutes. Then remove the cupcakes and cool on a rack.

For the icing, beat the pesto and cream cheese with an electric whisk until smooth and creamy. Smear the icing onto the cooled cupcakes and top with the cherry tomatoes.

Store without icing in an airtight container for up to 3 days, or freeze for up to 3 months.

Makes 1 dozen

pb & banana cupcakes

see variations page 236

This familiar combination makes a truly delicious cupcake.

for the cupcake
225 g (8 oz) unsalted butter, softened
200 g (7 oz) caster sugar
115 g (4 oz) self-raising flour
2 tsp baking powder
1 tsp salt
4 eggs
3 tbsp ground almonds
1 tsp vanilla essence
2 tsp cinnamon

4 tbsp peanut butter chips
250 g (9 oz) mashed bananas

for the icing
200 g (7 oz) cream cheese, softened
175 g (6 oz) icing sugar, sieved
1 tbsp lemon juice
1 tsp vanilla essence
115 g (4 oz) mashed banana

Preheat the oven to 175°C (350°F / Gas mark 4). Place 24 paper baking cases in muffin tins. Combine the butter, sugar, flour, baking powder, salt, eggs, almonds, vanilla and cinnamon in a large bowl and beat with an electric whisk until smooth and pale, about 2 to 3 minutes. Stir in the peanut butter chips and mashed banana. Spoon the batter into the paper cases. Bake for 20 minutes. Remove tin and cool for 5 minutes. Then remove the cupcakes and cool on a rack. To make the icing, beat the cream cheese and icing sugar in a medium bowl with an electric whisk until soft and light. Add the lemon juice, vanilla and mashed bananas. Beat until well combined. Spoon the icing over the cupcakes.

Store without icing in an airtight container for up to 2 days or freeze for up to 3 months.

Makes 2 dozen

ricotta cheesecake cupcakes

see variations page 237

Ricotta cheese is lower in fat than cream cheese and it has a great texture.

125 g (4½ oz) digestive biscuit crumbs
3 tbsp margarine, melted
2 tbsp honey
900 g (2 lb) semi-skimmed ricotta cheese
4 eggs

175 g (6 oz) icing sugar, sieved
1 tsp orange essence
75 g (3 oz) walnut halves

Preheat the oven to 160°C (325°F / Gas mark 3). Place 12 baking cases in a muffin tin.

In a food processor, combine the biscuit crumbs, margarine and honey. Spoon 1 tablespoon of the mixture into each case, pressing firmly into the bottom. Chill until set.

In a large bowl, beat the ricotta with an electric whisk until soft. Then beat in the eggs, icing sugar and orange essence. Spoon the mixture into the cases. Place a walnut on top of each cupcake.

Bake for 25 minutes. Remove tin from the oven and cool for 5 minutes. Then remove the cupcakes and cool on a rack. Chill until ready to serve.

Store covered in the refrigerator for up to 2 days.

Makes 1 dozen

low-fat vanilla cupcakes

see variations page 238

After you have used the seeds from the vanilla bean, put the pod into an airtight jar and pour caster sugar on top. In a few weeks you will have vanilla sugar!

for the cupcakes
3 egg yolks
225 g (8 oz) caster sugar
1 vanilla pod, seeds removed
50 ml (2 fl oz) cold water
115 g (4 oz) flour
1 tsp baking powder
pinch of salt

5 egg whites
1/8 tsp cream of tartar

for the glaze
175 g (6 oz) icing sugar
1 tsp vanilla essence
2 tbsp lemon juice
1 tbsp poppy seeds

Preheat the oven to 175°C (350°F / Gas mark 4). Place 12 paper baking cases in a muffin tin. In a large bowl, beat the egg yolks and half the sugar until pale and creamy. Then add the vanilla seeds. Add the water, flour, baking powder and salt to the egg mixture and beat with an electric whisk until just combined. In a medium bowl, combine the egg whites and cream of tartar. Beat with an electric whisk until soft peaks form. Add the remaining sugar, one-third at a time, beating well after each addition. Using a metal spoon, gently fold the egg whites into the batter. Spoon the mixture into the cases. Bake for 20 minutes. Remove and cool slightly. To make the glaze, sieve the icing sugar in a bowl. Add the vanilla essence, lemon juice and poppy seeds and beat until creamy and slightly runny. Drizzle the glaze over warm cupcakes. Store in an airtight container for up to 2 days, or freeze for up to 3 months.

Makes 1 dozen

flour-lite chocolate cupcakes

see variations page 239

This recipe has only a small amount of flour to give the cupcakes a light, fluffy texture.

50 g (2 oz) Dutch-process cocoa powder
150 g (5 oz) light brown sugar
3 tbsp plain flour
pinch of salt
1 tsp vanilla essence
1 tsp orange essence
175 ml (6 fl oz) skimmed milk

115 g (4 oz) plain chocolate, chopped
1 egg, lightly beaten
3 egg whites
$\frac{1}{4}$ tsp cream of tartar
75 g (3 oz) caster sugar
cocoa powder, for dusting
icing sugar, for dusting

In a heavy saucepan, combine the cocoa, sugar, flour, salt, vanilla, orange essence and milk over a gentle heat. Stir until the sugar dissolves, being careful not to burn the mixture. Remove from the heat, and gradually stir in the chocolate until it melts. Whisk in the egg. Transfer to a large bowl to cool, and set aside. Preheat the oven to 175°C (350°F / Gas mark 4). Place 12 paper baking cases in a muffin tin. In a medium bowl, combine the egg whites and cream of tartar. Beat with an electric whisk until soft peaks form. Gradually add the sugar, one-third at a time, beating for 1 minute after each addition. Using a metal spoon, fold the egg whites into the chocolate, making sure not to overmix. Spoon the mixture into the cases. Bake for 20 minutes. Remove the tin from the oven and cool for 5 minutes. Then remove the cupcakes, dust with cocoa powder and icing sugar, and serve immediately.

Store in an airtight container for up to 2 days, or freeze for up to 3 months.

Makes 1 dozen

quick apple sauce cupcakes

see variations page 240

Simple to make and low in fat, this recipe is based on the classic streusel cake.

for the cupcakes
115 g (4 oz) margarine, softened
150 g (5 oz) light brown sugar
1 egg, lightly beaten
175 g (6 oz) unsweetened apple sauce
225 g (8 oz) self-raising flour
1 tsp baking powder
1 tsp ground ginger
¼ tsp ground cloves

for the topping
30 g (1 oz) margarine, softened
30 g (1¼ oz) icing sugar, sieved
3 tbsp chopped walnuts
2 tbsp porridge oats
2 tbsp plain flour
½ tsp cinnamon

Preheat the oven to 175°C (350°F / Gas mark 4). Place 12 paper baking cases in a muffin tin. In a medium bowl, beat the margarine and sugar with an electric whisk until pale and creamy. Slowly add the egg and then the apple sauce, beating well after each addition. Add the flour, baking powder and spices, mixing until just combined. To make the topping, combine all the ingredients in a small bowl. Mix with a fork until the topping resembles coarse breadcrumbs. Set aside. Spoon the batter into the cases. Sprinkle some topping on each cupcake and bake for 20 to 25 minutes. Remove tin from the oven and cool for 5 minutes. Then remove the cupcakes and cool on a rack.

Store in an airtight container for up to 3 days, or freeze for up to 3 months.

Makes 1 dozen

glazed blueberry-lime cupcakes

see variations page 241

Low in fat with super-food blueberries – you may feel virtuous when you bake these!

for the cupcakes
115 g (4 oz) margarine, softened
225 g (8 oz) caster sugar
2 eggs, lightly beaten
1 tsp vanilla essence
115 ml (4 fl oz) skimmed milk
225 g (4 oz) self-raising flour
1 tsp baking powder

115 g (4 oz) fresh blueberries
1 tbsp grated lime zest

for the glaze
115 g (4 oz) caster sugar
2 tbsp grated lime zest
3 tbsp lime juice
2 tbsp boiling water

Preheat the oven to 175°C (350°F / Gas mark 4). Place 18 paper baking cases in muffin tins. Combine the margarine and sugar with an electric whisk until soft and creamy. Add the eggs slowly and mix well. Beat in the vanilla and milk. Sieve the flour and baking powder and stir into the batter until just combined. Fold in the blueberries and lime zest. Spoon the mixture into the cases. Bake for 20 minutes. Remove tins from the oven and cool for 5 minutes. Then remove the cupcakes and cool on a rack. To make the glaze, mix the sugar, lime zest, lime juice and boiling water in a small saucepan. Bring to a gentle simmer over a medium heat, stirring to dissolve the sugar. Simmer uncovered for 5 minutes. Remove from the heat, cool slightly, and spoon over the cool cupcakes. Store in an airtight container for up to 3 days, or unglazed in the freezer for up to 3 months.

Makes 1½ dozen

banana & honey cupcakes

see variations page 242

Bananas lend themselves to natural sweeteners like maple syrup and honey. Add walnuts to offset the sweetness and to give the cupcakes a little crunch.

450 g (1 lb) mashed bananas
150 g (5 oz) light brown sugar
100 g (3½ oz) honey
50 g (2 oz) margarine, melted

115 g (4 oz) self-raising flour
1 tsp baking powder
pinch of salt
150 g (5 oz) walnuts, roughly chopped

Preheat the oven to 175°C (350°F / Gas mark 4). Place 18 paper baking cases in muffin tins.

In a large bowl, combine the bananas, sugar, honey and margarine. Beat with an electric whisk until well blended. Slowly add the flour, baking powder and salt, and mix well. Fold in the chopped walnuts.

Spoon the batter into the cases. Bake for 20 minutes. Remove tins from the oven and cool for 5 minutes. Remove the cupcakes and cool on a rack. Place each in a foil cup to display.

Store in an airtight container for up to 2 days, or freeze for up to 3 months.

Makes 1½ dozen

marbled mini bundt cakes

see variations page 243

Bake these cakes in little bundt pans for a really extravagant-looking cupcake. You can also use ordinary muffin tins.

115 g (4 oz) margarine, softened
225 g (8 oz) caster sugar
2 eggs, lightly beaten
1 tsp vanilla essence
175 g (6 oz) plain flour
1 tbsp baking powder

175 ml (6 fl oz) skimmed milk
2 tbsp Dutch-process cocoa powder
100 g (3½ oz) plain chocolate, finely chopped
cocoa powder for dusting

Preheat the oven to 175°C (350°F / Gas mark 4). Grease 6 mini bundt tins or a large 6-cup muffin tin. In a large bowl, beat the margarine and sugar with an electric whisk until thick and pale. Slowly add the eggs and vanilla, beating well. Mix the flour and baking powder in a medium bowl. Add to the margarine mixture in thirds, alternating with the milk.

Divide the batter into two bowls. Fold the cocoa powder and chocolate into one of the bowls. Spoon a little plain batter into the bottom of each bundt tin, then spoon some chocolate batter on top. Continue until each tin is three-quarters full and there are 4 layers. Swirl the mixture in each tin using the point of a knife. Bake for 35 minutes. Remove tins from the oven and cool for 10 minutes. Then remove the bundt cakes and cool on a rack. Serve dusted with cocoa powder.

Store in an airtight container for up to 2 days.

Makes ½ dozen

low-fat carrot & nut cupcakes

see variations page 244

The low-fat version of the classic American cake. If you can't get fat-free cream cheese for the icing, use fat-free plain yoghurt.

for the cupcakes
225 g (8 oz) self-raising flour
1 tsp baking powder
$^1/_2$ tsp nutmeg
1 tsp ground ginger
150 g (5 oz) brown sugar
100 g ($3^1/_2$ oz) grated carrot
100 g ($3^1/_2$ oz) walnuts, roughly chopped
200 g (7 oz) mashed bananas

2 eggs, lightly beaten
175 ml (6 fl oz) vegetable oil

for the icing
200 g (7 oz) fat-free cream cheese, softened
115 g (4 oz) icing sugar, sieved
1 tsp vanilla essence
4 tbsp chopped walnuts
12 walnut halves

Preheat the oven to 175°C (350°F / Gas mark 4). Place 12 paper baking cases in a muffin tin. In a large bowl, combine all the cupcake ingredients. Beat on a low speed with an electric whisk until all the ingredients are combined. Spoon the mixture into the cases. Bake for 20 minutes. Remove tin from the oven and cool for 5 minutes. Remove the cupcakes and cool on a rack. To make the icing, combine the cream cheese with the icing sugar and vanilla with an electric whisk. Beat until smooth and creamy. Fold in the walnuts. Smear onto the cooled cupcakes and garnish with the walnut halves.

Store without icing in an airtight container for up to 3 days, or freeze for up to 3 months.

Makes 1 dozen

ultimate flourless choc cupcakes

see variations page 245

For maximum luxury, top with chocolate cream.

for the cupcakes
300 g (10½ oz) plain chocolate chips
225 g (8 oz) unsalted butter
4 eggs
4 egg yolks
115 g (4 oz) caster sugar
2 tbsp Dutch-process cocoa powder, sieved
2 tbsp ground almonds
1 tsp vanilla essence

for the icing
2 tbsp Dutch-process cocoa powder
4 tbsp icing sugar
350 ml (12 fl oz) double cream
1 tsp vanilla essence
½ tsp orange essence

Preheat the oven to 190°C (375°F / Gas mark 5). Place 12 paper baking cases in a muffin tin. Put the chocolate and butter in a medium bowl over a pan of simmering water, and stir until completely melted. Set aside to cool. In a large bowl, cream the eggs, yolks and sugar with an electric whisk until pale and thick. Gently fold in the melted chocolate and remaining ingredients. Spoon the batter into the cases. Bake for 20 minutes. Remove tin from the oven and cool for 5 minutes. Then remove the cupcakes and cool on a rack. To make the icing, sieve the cocoa and icing sugar together into a medium bowl. Add the cream, vanilla and orange essence. Beat until soft, but.the cream should still hold its shape. Spoon over the warm cupcakes.

Store without icing in an airtight container for up to 2 days.

Makes 1 dozen

chocolate vegan cupcakes

see variations page 246

To make this authentically vegan, you must use specially labelled vegan chocolate chips.

275 g (10 oz) plain flour
4 tbsp Dutch-process cocoa powder
pinch of salt
450 g (1 lb oz) caster sugar
100 g (3$\frac{1}{2}$ oz) unsweetened apple sauce

450 ml (16 fl oz) cold water
2 tsp white vinegar
2 tsp bicarbonate of soda
175 g (6 oz) vegan plain chocolate chips
cocoa powder for dusting

Preheat the oven to 190°C (375°F / Gas mark 5). Place 12 paper baking cases in a muffin tin. Sieve the flour, cocoa, salt and sugar into a large bowl and set aside.

In a separate large bowl, combine the apple sauce, water, vinegar and bicarbonate of soda. Add the flour mixture and stir well to combine. Fold in the chocolate chips.

Spoon the mixture into the cases. Bake for about 20 minutes. Remove tin from the oven and cool for 5 minutes. Then remove the cupcakes and cool on a rack.

Serve dusted with cocoa.

Store in an airtight container for up to 3 days, or freeze for up to 3 months.

Makes 1 dozen

g.i. carrot cupcakes

see variations page 247

These cupcakes are perfect for those using the glycaemic index to monitor their diet. Low glycaemic foods release their sugars slowly – and are thus more beneficial for maintaining blood sugar levels.

115 ml (4 fl oz) light vegetable oil
115 g (4 oz) brown sugar
1 egg, lightly beaten
3 egg whites
190 g (6½ oz) grated carrot
190 g (6½ oz) grated cooking apples
225 g (8 oz) raisins

115 g (4 oz) dates, chopped
115 g (4 oz) mixed dried berries
115 g (4 oz) walnuts, chopped
1 tsp mixed spice
1 tsp baking powder
350 g (12 oz) self-raising wholemeal flour

Preheat the oven to 175°C (350°F / Gas mark 4). Place 12 paper baking cases into a muffin tin. In a large bowl, combine the oil and sugar, and beat with an electric whisk until light and smooth, about 2 to 3 minutes. Beat the egg and egg whites, one at a time, and then add the carrots, apples, dried fruits and walnuts. Sieve the rest of the ingredients into a medium mixing bowl. Add them to the carrot mixture, stirring until just combined. Spoon the mixture into the cases. Bake for 20 minutes. Remove tin from the oven and cool for 5 minutes. Then remove the cupcakes and cool on a rack. Serve with a low-fat margarine spread.

Store in an airtight container for up to 3 days, or freeze for up to 3 months.

Makes 1 dozen

dairy-free berry cupcakes

see variations page 248

These little treats are wonderful for the lactose-intolerant cupcake lover.

for the cupcakes
375 g (13 oz) mixed fresh berries (blueberries,
   strawberries, cranberries, blackberries)
225 g (8 oz) flour
115 g (4 oz) brown sugar
1 tbsp baking powder

4 tbsp vegetable oil
2 eggs, lightly beaten

for the topping
125 g (4½ oz) mixed berry jam

Preheat the oven to 175°C (350°F / Gas mark 4). Place 12 paper baking cases into a muffin tin. In a food processor, purée 240 g (8½ oz) of the berries until smooth. In a small bowl, lightly crush the reserved berries with a fork. In a medium bowl, mix the flour, sugar and baking powder. In a large bowl, beat the oil and eggs. Add the puréed berries and mix well. Stir in the flour mixture until combined. Fold in the crushed berries.

Spoon the batter into the cases. Top each cupcake with a teaspoon of jam. Bake for 20 minutes. Remove tin from the oven and cool for 5 minutes. Then remove the cupcakes and cool on a rack.

Store in an airtight container for up to 3 days, or freeze for up to 3 months.

Makes 1 dozen

gluten-free pecan cupcakes

see variations page 249

Gluten-free flour has a variety of uses. Look for it in speciality food or health shops. Add a little more liquid than you would when using normal flour, since it will be absorbed.

300 g (10½ oz) gluten-free plain flour
175 g (6 oz) caster sugar
1½ tbsp baking powder
pinch of salt
2 eggs, lightly beaten

50 g (2 oz) unsalted butter, melted
300 ml (10½ fl oz) milk
1 tsp vanilla essence
150 g (5 oz) pecans, roughly chopped
100 g (3½ oz) dates, chopped

Preheat the oven to 200°C (400°F / Gas mark 6). Grease a 12-cup muffin tin.

In a medium bowl, mix the flour, sugar, baking powder and salt. In a large bowl, beat the eggs, butter, milk and vanilla. Add the dry ingredients and stir until nearly combined. Fold in the pecans and dates.

Spoon the mixture into the prepared tin. Bake for 20 minutes. Remove tin from the oven and cool for 5 minutes. Then remove the muffins and cool on a rack.

Store in an airtight container for up to 3 days, or freeze for up to 3 months.

Makes 1 dozen

mini couscous cakes

see base recipe page 209

mini couscous & coriander cakes
Prepare the basic cupcake recipe, adding 2 tablespoons freshly chopped coriander along with the lemon zest and parsley.

mini couscous cakes with preserved lemon & thyme
Prepare the basic cupcake recipe, adding 1 teaspoon chopped preserved lemon and 1 tablespoon chopped thyme leaves along with the lemon zest and parsley.

mini couscous cakes with olive & chilli
Prepare the basic cupcake recipe, adding 3 tablespoons tapenade or olive paste and 1 teaspoon chopped chilli pepper along with the lemon zest and parsley.

mini couscous cakes with jalapeño
Prepare the basic cupcake recipe, adding 2 tablespoons finely chopped canned jalapeños in adobo, and substituting lime for lemon zest and chopped coriander for parsley.

basil pesto cupcakes

see base recipe page 210

basil pesto & coriander cupcakes
Prepare the basic cupcake recipe, adding 3 tablespoons finely chopped coriander to the icing.

red pepper pesto cupcakes
Prepare the basic cupcake recipe, substituting 115 g (4 oz) red pepper pesto for the basil pesto.

basil pesto & chilli cupcakes
Prepare the basic cupcake recipe, adding 1 teaspoon chilli flakes to the batter before it has been mixed together.

horseradish & bacon cupcakes
Prepare the basic cupcake recipe, adding 2 strips crisply cooked and chopped bacon to the batter before it has been mixed together. For the icing, substitute 2 teaspoons prepared horseradish for the pesto and 60 g (2 oz) chopped spring onions for the tomatoes.

southwest-style cornbread cupcakes
Prepare the basic cupcake recipe, adding 1 small chopped jalapeño pepper to the batter before it has been mixed together. For the icing, substitute salsa for the pesto and 8 tablespoons chopped coriander for the tomatoes.

pb & banana cupcakes

see base recipe page 212

banana & pecan cupcakes
Prepare the basic cupcake recipe, substituting 4 tablespoons of chopped pecans for the peanut butter chips.

pb & banana cupcakes with maple syrup & ginger icing
Prepare the basic cupcake recipe. For the icing, substitute 4 tablespoons maple syrup for the icing sugar. Stir in 3 tablespoons chopped crystallised ginger along with the peanut butter chips and mashed banana.

pb, banana & chocolate chip cupcakes
Prepare the basic cupcake recipe, adding 4 tablespoons of plain chocolate chips after creaming the batter.

pb, banana & blueberry cupcakes
Prepare the basic cupcake recipe, adding 4 tablespoons of dried blueberries after creaming the batter.

pb & pumpkin cupcakes
Prepare the basic cupcake recipe, substituting 170 g (6 oz) tinned pumpkin for the banana.

ricotta cheesecake cupcakes

see base recipe page 215

banana & raisin ricotta cheesecake cupcakes

Prepare the basic recipe but use only 750 g (1 lb 10 oz) ricotta cheese. Add
225 g (8 oz) mashed bananas to the ricotta cheese after adding the eggs
and icing sugar. Add 75 g (3 oz) raisins along with the walnuts.

blueberry–ricotta cheesecake cupcakes

Prepare the basic cheesecake mixture, folding in 150 g (5 oz) fresh
blueberries just before adding the walnuts.

raspberry & lime ricotta cheesecake cupcakes

Prepare the basic cheesecake mixture, folding in 150 g (5 oz) fresh
raspberries and 1 tablespoon freshly grated lime zest just before adding
the walnuts.

pumpkin cheesecake cupcakes

Prepare the basic recipe but use only 750 g (1 lb 10 oz) ricotta cheese. Add
145 g (5 oz) tinned pumpkin pie filling to the ricotta cheese after adding the
eggs and icing sugar. Omit the orange essence and the walnuts.

variations

low-fat vanilla cupcakes

see base recipe page 216

low-fat cupcakes with fennel & orange drizzle
Prepare the basic cupcake mixture. In the glaze, substitute 2 teaspoons
lightly crushed fennel seeds for the poppy seeds, and substitute
1 teaspoon orange essence for the vanilla essence.

low-fat cupcakes with strawberry & lime drizzle
Prepare the basic cupcake mixture. In the glaze, substitute 1 teaspoon
strawberry essence for the vanilla, and add 1 tablespoon freshly grated
lime zest to the mixture.

low-fat cupcakes with almond & cherry drizzle
Prepare the basic cupcake mixture. In the glaze, substitute 1 teaspoon
almond essence for the vanilla essence. Add 2 tablespoons chopped
crystallised cherries.

low-fat cappuccino cupcakes
Prepare the basic cupcake mixture, adding 1 teaspoon cinnamon. In the
glaze, substitute freshly brewed dark coffee for the lemon juice. Omit the
poppy seeds. Decorate with chocolate sprinkles.

flour–lite chocolate cupcakes

see base recipe page 217

flour–lite chocolate & orange cupcakes
Prepare the basic cupcake recipe, substituting 2 teaspoons orange essence for the vanilla essence.

flour–lite chocolate-glazed cupcakes
Prepare the basic cupcake recipe. Make a glaze: Sieve 175 g (6 oz) icing sugar and 2 tablespoons Dutch-process cocoa powder into a medium bowl. Beat 2 tablespoons softened margarine into the cocoa powder mixture, adding 1 tablespoon warm water and 1 tablespoon coffee liqueur to make a pourable consistency. Spoon over the cupcakes.

flour–lite chocolate & cinnamon cupcakes
Prepare the basic cupcake recipe, adding 2 teaspoons cinnamon to the dry ingredients.

flour–lite chocolate & chilli cupcakes
Prepare the basic cupcake recipe, adding 2 teaspoons ground dried chilli to the dry ingredients.

variations

quick apple sauce cupcakes

see base recipe page 218

quick apple sauce & pecan cupcakes
Prepare the basic cupcake recipe, adding 3 tablespoons chopped pecans after adding the dry ingredients. For the topping, substitute 3 tablespoons chopped pecans for the walnuts.

quick apple sauce & raisin cupcakes
Prepare the basic cupcake recipe, adding 4 tablespoons raisins after adding the dry ingredients.

quick apple sauce & cranberry cupcakes
Prepare the basic cupcake recipe, adding 4 tablespoons dried cranberries after adding the dry ingredients.

quick apple sauce & black walnut cupcakes
Prepare the basic cupcake recipe, adding 3 tablespoons chopped black walnuts after adding the dry ingredients. For the topping, substitute 3 tablespoons chopped black walnuts for the walnuts.

variations

glazed blueberry–lime cupcakes

see base recipe page 219

glazed raspberry–lemon cupcakes
Prepare the basic cupcake recipe, substituting 150 g (5 oz) fresh raspberries
for the blueberries, and 1 tablespoon grated lemon zest for the lime zest in
the glaze.

glazed blackberry–orange cupcakes
Prepare the basic cupcake recipe, substituting 150 g (5 oz) fresh blackberries
for the blueberries, and 1 tablespoon grated orange zest for the lime zest in
the glaze.

glazed strawberry–lime cupcakes
Prepare the basic cupcake recipe, substituting 150 g (5 oz) fresh sliced
strawberries for the blueberries.

glazed coconut–lime cupcakes
Prepare the basic cupcake recipe, substituting 75 g (2½ oz) desiccated
coconut for the blueberries.

variations

banana & honey cupcakes

see base recipe page 221

banana, hazelnut & honey cupcakes
Prepare the basic cupcake recipe, substituting 115 g (4 oz) roughly chopped unblanched hazelnuts for the walnuts.

banana & maple syrup cupcakes
Prepare the basic cupcake recipe, substituting 100 g (3½ oz) maple syrup for the honey.

banana, pecan & golden syrup cupcakes
Prepare the basic cupcake recipe, substituting 115 g (4 oz) roughly chopped pecans for the walnuts, and 100 g (3½ oz) golden syrup for the honey.

banana, honey & blueberry cupcakes
Prepare the basic cupcake recipe, substituting 145 g (5 oz) dried blueberries for the walnuts.

marbled mini bundt cakes

see base recipe page 222

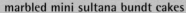

marbled mini sultana bundt cakes
Prepare the basic cupcake recipe. After dividing the batters, add
3 tablespoons sultanas to the plain batter.

marbled mini orange & walnut bundt cakes
Prepare the basic cupcake recipe. After dividing the batters, add 1 teaspoon
orange essence to the chocolate batter, and 3 tablespoons chopped walnuts
to the plain batter.

marbled mini pistachio bundt cakes
Prepare the basic cupcake recipe. After dividing the batters, add
3 tablespoons chopped pistachio nuts to the plain batter.

marbled mini chocolate orange bundt cakes
Prepare the basic cupcake recipe. After dividing the batters, add 1 teaspoon
orange essence to the chocolate batter, and 3 tablespoons chopped
crystallised orange to the plain batter.

variations

low-fat carrot & nut cupcakes

see base recipe page 224

low-fat carrot & pecan cupcakes
Prepare the basic cupcake mixture, substituting 75 g (3 oz) roughly
chopped pecans for the walnuts. Substitute 4 tablespoons chopped
pecans for the walnuts in the icing, and substitute 12 pecans for the
walnut halves for garnishing.

low-fat ginger-iced carrot cupcakes
Prepare the basic cupcake mixture. For the icing, substitute 3 tablespoons
chopped crystallised ginger for the chopped walnuts.

low-fat carrot & orange cupcakes
Prepare the basic cupcake mixture, adding 1 teaspoon orange essence and
1 teaspoon ground cumin to the cupcakes.

low-fat carrot, courgette & yellow squash cupcakes
Prepare the basic cupcake mixture, substituting 2 tablespoons grated
courgette and 2 tablespoons grated yellow squash for 30 g (1 oz)
of the carrots.

variations

ultimate flourless choc cupcakes

see base recipe page 226

ultimate flourless peppermint cream cupcakes
Prepare the basic cupcake recipe. Substitute 1 teaspoon peppermint essence for the vanilla and orange essence.

ultimate flourless vanilla ice cream cupcakes
Prepare the basic cupcake recipe. Make an ice cream topping: Mix 450 ml (16 fl oz) ready-made custard and 300 ml (10 fl oz) whipping cream in a large bowl, and beat well. Add 1 teaspoon vanilla essence. Pour into an ice cream maker and churn until frozen. Put 1 scoop on top of each cupcake.

ultimate flourless strawberry cream cupcakes
Prepare the basic cupcake recipe. For the icing, substitute 1 teaspoon strawberry essence for the vanilla essence. Fold in 100 g (3½ oz) finely chopped fresh strawberries after beating the cream.

ultimate flourless coffee cream cupcakes
Prepare the basic cupcake recipe. Substitute 1 teaspoon coffee essence for the vanilla and orange essence.

variations

chocolate vegan cupcakes

see base recipe page 227

chocolate & orange vegan cupcakes
Prepare the basic cupcake recipe, adding 1¹/₂ tablespoons grated orange zest to the mixture along with the chocolate chips.

chocolate & hazelnut vegan cupcakes
Prepare the basic cupcake recipe, adding 75 g (3 oz) chopped roasted hazelnuts along with the chocolate chips.

chocolate & coffee vegan cupcakes
Prepare the basic cupcake recipe, adding 50 ml (2 fl oz) hot coffee to the apple sauce mixture.

chocolate & ginger vegan cupcakes
Prepare the basic cupcake recipe, adding 2 tablespoons grated fresh ginger to the apple sauce mixture.

variations

g.i. carrot cupcakes

see base recipe page 228

g.i. pecan cupcakes
Prepare the basic cupcake mixture, substituting 115 g (4 oz) chopped pecans for the walnuts.

g.i. banana cupcakes
Prepare the basic cupcake mixture, adding 125 g (4½ oz) mashed bananas along with the carrots and fruits. Substitute ½ teaspoon nutmeg for the mixed spice.

g.i. currant cupcakes
Prepare the basic cupcake mixture, substituting 200 g (7 oz) currants for the raisins.

g.i. apricot–almond cupcakes
Prepare the basic cupcake mixture, substituting 200 g (7 oz) chopped dried apricots for the raisins and 60 g (2 oz) chopped almonds for the walnuts.

dairy-free berry cupcakes

see base recipe page 230

dairy-free apple & berry cupcakes
Prepare the basic cupcake recipe, substituting 240 g (8¹/₂ oz) unsweetened apple sauce for 240 g (8¹/₂ oz) of the mixed berries.

dairy-free pear & berry cupcakes
Prepare the basic cupcake recipe, substituting 240 g (8¹/₂ oz) puréed tinned pears for 240 g (8¹/₂ oz) of the mixed berries. Add 1 teaspoon almond essence to the batter.

dairy-free peach & berry cupcakes
Prepare the basic cupcake recipe, substituting 240 g (8¹/₂ oz) puréed tinned peaches for 240 g (8¹/₂ oz) of the mixed berries.

dairy-free apricot cupcakes
Prepare the basic cupcake recipe, substituting 240 g (8¹/₂ oz) chopped, tinned apricots for the mixed berries. For the topping, substitute 170 g (6 oz) apricot jam for the mixed berry jam.

variations

gluten-free pecan cupcakes

see base recipe page 232

gluten-free mixed peel cupcakes
Prepare the basic cupcake recipe, substituting 100 g (3½ oz) chopped crystallised mixed peel for the dates.

gluten-free apricot cupcakes
Prepare the basic cupcake recipe, substituting 100 g (3½ oz) chopped dried apricots for the dates.

gluten-free molasses cupcakes
Prepare the basic cupcake recipe, omitting the sugar and adding 4 tablespoons molasses and 4 tablespoons honey to the milk mixture.

gluten-free sorghum cupcakes
Prepare the basic cupcake recipe, omitting the sugar and adding 75 g (3 oz) sorghum to the milk mixture.

designer cupcakes

A few artful twists can take cupcakes to a new, fun level. Designer Buttercream Icing, Mouldable White Chocolate, cookies and sweets make decorating easy.

designer buttercream

This light and fluffy icing can be flavoured and tinted any way you wish, and will keep, covered, in the refrigerator for a week, or frozen for several months.

225 g (8 oz) unsalted butter, softened
115 g (4 oz) vegetable shortening
4 egg whites
2 tsp lemon juice

$^1/_2$ teaspoon cream of tartar
100 g (3$^1/_2$ oz) sugar
60 ml (4 tbsp) water
2 tsp vanilla essence

Beat the butter and shortening together in a food processor until smooth; set aside in a cool area.

Using a stand mixer, beat the egg whites with the lemon juice, salt and cream of tartar until soft peaks form; set aside. Stir the sugar and water together in a saucepan until the sugar has dissolved. Cook over medium-high heat until a sugar thermometer inserted in the syrup registers 120°C (250°F), about 10 minutes.

Pour the hot syrup in a thin stream into the beaten egg whites, beating constantly at low speed, until you have a thick, glossy icing. Beat in the vanilla. Continue beating on medium speed until the bottom of bowl is as warm as your face, about 36°C (98°F). Set aside to cool for 5 minutes.

Switch to the paddle attachment and add the butter mixture, 2 tablespoons at a time, beating well after each addition until smooth and creamy. If the icing breaks, continue beating at low to medium speed and the mixture will come back together. Cool for about an hour before using.

day at the beach

see variations page 272

Roll out the striped towel, open the parasol and enjoy the waves lapping at the beach — all in miniature on top of the cupcake.

for the cupcakes
225 g (8 oz) unsalted butter, softened
225 g (8 oz) caster sugar
225 g (8 oz) self-raising flour
2 tsp baking powder
1 tsp salt
4 eggs
115 ml (4 fl oz) buttermilk
1½ tsp vanilla essence

for the icing & decorations
1 recipe Designer Buttercream (page 251)
A few drops of food colouring
225 g (8 oz) digestive biscuit crumbs
18 cocktail parasols
18 fruit-striped sweets, cut into 2-inch pieces

Preheat the oven to 175°C (350°F / Gas mark 4). Place 18 paper baking cases in muffin tins. Place all the ingredients in a medium bowl and beat with an electric whisk until smooth and pale, about 2 to 3 minutes. Spoon the mixture into the cases. Bake for 20 minutes or until a skewer inserted in the centre comes out clean. Remove the tins from the oven and cool for 5 minutes. Then remove the cupcakes and cool on a rack.

Leave ⅔ of the buttercream white. Tint the other ⅓ ocean blue. For each cupcake: Ice ⅔ of the top with white buttercream and sprinkle with digestive biscuit crumbs for the beach. Ice the other ⅓ with blue buttercream, creating 'waves' with a knife. Lay the sweet on the diagonal across the 'sand' for a beach towel and insert the parasol at an angle to make the beach umbrella.

Makes 1½ dozen

daisy daze

see variations page 273

Snipped-on-the-diagonal miniature marshmallows, cut sides dipped in coloured sugar, form the petals on these flowery cupcakes.

for the cupcakes
225 g (8 oz) unsalted butter, softened
115 g (4 oz) caster sugar
225 g (8 oz) self-raising flour
2 tsp baking powder
1 tsp salt
4 eggs
115 ml (4 fl oz) buttermilk
1½ tsp vanilla essence

for the icing & decorations
1 recipe Designer Buttercream (page 251)
yellow food colouring
225 g (8 oz) miniature marshmallows
18 lemon gumdrops, lemon balls or other small, circular lemon sweets
yellow decorating sugar

Preheat the oven to 175°C (350°F / Gas mark 4). Place 18 paper baking cases in muffin tins. Place all the ingredients in a medium bowl and beat with an electric whisk until smooth and pale, about 2 to 3 minutes. Spoon the mixture into the cases. Bake for 20 minutes or until a skewer inserted in the centre comes out clean.

Remove the tins from the oven and cool for 5 minutes. Then remove the cupcakes and cool on a rack.

Tint the buttercream yellow. For each cupcake: Ice the top. Place a lemon gumdrop in the centre. Snip each miniature marshmallow in half lengthwise, press cut side in yellow sugar and arrange sugared side up around the gumdrop like petals.

Makes 1½ dozen

clown

see variations page 274

These colourful cupcakes could be a big hit at a children's party. Choose sugar cones with a pointed end.

for the cupcakes
225 g (8 oz) unsalted butter, softened
115 g (4 oz) caster sugar
225 g (8 oz) self-raising flour
2 tsp baking powder
1 tsp salt
4 eggs
115 ml (4 fl oz) buttermilk
1½ tsp vanilla essence

for the icing & decorations
1 recipe Designer Buttercream (page 251)
900 g (2 lb) white chocolate chips
icing sugar, for dusting
18 sugar cones with pointed ends
coloured sprinkles
1 recipe Mouldable White Chocolate (page 15)
red food colouring

Preheat the oven to 175°C (350°F / Gas mark 4). Place 18 paper baking cases in muffin tins. Place all the ingredients in a medium bowl and beat with an electric whisk until smooth and pale, about 2 to 3 minutes. Spoon the mixture into the cases. Bake for 20 minutes or until a skewer inserted in the centre comes out clean. Remove the tins from the oven and cool for 5 minutes. Then remove the cupcakes and cool on a rack. For each cupcake: Ice the top. Melt the white chocolate chips. Lightly brush it over the outside of each sugar cone and roll in coloured sprinkles. Let set. Tint Mouldable White Chocolate red, divide it into 18 pieces. Pinch off a small portion from each piece and roll into a ball. Roll the rest of the piece into a 40-cm (16-in) rope on a icing sugar-dusted surface. Place the sugar cone firmly in the centre of each cupcake and secure the red ball on the pointed end. Loop the rope around the circumference of the cone to make clown hair. Scatter more coloured sprinkles on the icing.

Makes 1 ½ dozen

spider's web

see variations page 275

Inject a little mystery into your cupcake art.

for the cupcakes
225 g (8 oz) unsalted butter, softened
115 g (4 oz) caster sugar
225 g (8 oz) self-raising flour
2 tsp baking powder
1 tsp salt
4 eggs
115 ml (4 fl oz) buttermilk
1½ tsp vanilla essence

for the icing & decorations
1 recipe Designer Buttercream (page 251)
black gel icing
18 licorice gumdrops
18 black craft pipe cleaners or chenille sticks

Preheat the oven to 175°C (350°F / Gas mark 4). Place 18 paper baking cases in muffin tins. Place all the ingredients in a medium bowl and beat with an electric whisk until smooth and pale, about 2 to 3 minutes. Spoon the mixture into the cases. Bake for 20 minutes or until a skewer inserted in the centre comes out clean.

Remove the tins from the oven and cool for 5 minutes. Then remove the cupcakes and cool on a rack.

For each cupcake: Ice the top. Using a black gel icing tube, draw three concentric circles radiating out from the centre of the cupcake. With a knife, draw across the icing in four places to create the web. Place a large licorice gumdrop in the centre of the cupcake. Cut each pipe cleaner into 8 pieces and fold in half to create legs. Arrange around the gumdrop.

Makes 1½ dozen

how does your garden grow?

see variations page 276

Even if you don't have green fingers, you can still have a garden atop a cupcake.

for the cupcakes
225 g (8 oz) unsalted butter, softened
115 g (4 oz) caster sugar
225 g (8 oz) self-raising flour
1 tsp baking powder
1/2 tsp salt
4 eggs
115 ml (4 fl oz) buttermilk
1 tsp vanilla essence

for the icing & decorations
100 g (3 1/2 oz) plain chocolate, roughly chopped
2 tbsp milk
60 g (2 oz) unsalted butter
100 g (3 1/2 oz) icing sugar, sieved
300 g (10 1/2 oz) chocolate bourbons, crushed
170 g (6 oz) desiccated coconut tinted green
340 g (12 oz) ready-to-roll white fondant icing
brown, orange and green food colouring
18 toothpicks

Preheat the oven to 175°C (350°F / Gas mark 4). Place 18 paper baking cases into muffin tins. Combine all the cupcake ingredients in a medium bowl and beat with an electric whisk until smooth and pale, about 2 to 3 minutes. Spoon the batter into the cases. Bake for 20 minutes. Remove the tins from the oven and cool for 5 minutes. Remove the cupcakes and cool on the rack. To make the icing, gently heat the chocolate, milk and butter in a small, heavy saucepan, stirring until melted. Remove from the heat and beat in the icing sugar. Ice the top of each cupcake, and sprinkle with bourbon crumbs. Arrange two parallel rows of green coconut. Split the fondant icing into thirds, and tint each a different colour. Shape carrots and cauliflowers from orange and green fondant icing, and arrange on top of each cupcake. Shape a shovel from brown icing – use a toothpick to support the shaft, and also to position the shovel on each cupcake.

Makes 1 1/2 dozen

bride doll

see variations page 277

For a little girl's birthday party or a bridal shower, these doll cupcakes can be customised with icing colours and decorations. Mini dolls on picks are available at craft stores and cake decorating shops.

for the cupcakes
225 g (8 oz) unsalted butter, softened
115 g (4 oz) caster sugar
225 g (8 oz) self-raising flour
2 tsp baking powder
1 tsp salt
4 eggs
115 ml (4 fl oz) buttermilk
1¹/₂ tsp vanilla essence

for the icing & decorations
2 recipes Designer Buttercream (page 251)
18 mini dolls on picks
sugar pearls
white sugar flowers

Preheat the oven to 175°C (350°F / Gas mark 4). Place 18 paper baking cases in muffin tins. Place all the ingredients in a medium bowl and beat with an electric whisk until smooth and pale, about 2 to 3 minutes. Spoon the mixture into the cases. Bake for 20 minutes or until a skewer inserted in the centre comes out clean. Remove the tins from the oven and cool for 5 minutes. Then remove the cupcakes and cool on a rack. When cool, remove the cupcake wrappers and turn the cupcakes upside down. Reserve ¹/₃ of the buttercream.

For each cupcake: Ice the top. Insert a doll in the centre. Spoon the reserved buttercream into a piping bag or a sealable plastic bag with an end corner snipped, and pipe it to form a strapless bodice on each doll. Create a pattern on each dress using sugar pearls and flowers.

Makes 1¹/₂ dozen

ruffles & pearls

see variations page 278

Roll out, roll up, and form stunning fondant roses to top each cupcake for an elegant finish.

for the cupcakes
225 g (8 oz) unsalted butter, softened
115 g (4 oz) caster sugar
225 g (8 oz) self-raising flour
2 tsp baking powder
1 tsp salt
4 eggs
115 ml (4 fl oz) buttermilk
1½ tsp vanilla essence

for the icing & decorations
1 recipe Designer Buttercream (page 251)
1 recipe Mouldable White Chocolate (page 15)
icing sugar, for dusting
white sugar pearls

Preheat the oven to 175°C (350°F / Gas mark 4). Place 18 paper baking cases in muffin tins. Place all the ingredients in a medium bowl and beat with an electric whisk until smooth and pale, about 2 to 3 minutes. Spoon the mixture into the cases. Bake for 20 minutes or until a skewer inserted in the centre comes out clean. Remove the tins from the oven and cool for 5 minutes. Then remove the cupcakes and cool on a rack.

Divide the Mouldable White Chocolate into 9 pieces. On a flat surface dusted with icing sugar, dust each piece with the sugar and roll out to a 40-cm (16-in) oval. Starting at a long end and using a metal spatula, roll it up. Cut the roll in half in the middle to form 2, 5-cm (2½-in) ruffled pieces. For each cupcake: Ice the top with white buttercream. Place the cut side of a ruffled piece in the centre and gently spread the ruffles. Sprinkle with sugar pearls.

Makes 1½ dozen

morning latte

see variations page 279

The morning cup of java just got a little sweeter – and more interesting! Coordinate the colour of the pipe cleaner 'handles' with the colours of your cupcake paper liners.

for the cupcakes
225 g (8 oz) unsalted butter, softened
115 g (4 oz) caster sugar
225 g (8 oz) self-raising flour
1 tsp baking powder
$^1/_2$ tsp salt
4 eggs
1 tsp vanilla essence

for the icing & decorations
100 g (3$^1/_2$ oz) plain chocolate, roughly chopped
2 tbsp freshly brewed dark coffee
60 g (2 oz) unsalted butter
100 g (3$^1/_2$ oz) icing sugar, sieved
215-g (7$^1/_2$-oz) jar Marshmallow Fluff or 200 g
    (7 oz) mini marshmallows, melted
18 craft pipe cleaners or chenille sticks

Preheat the oven to 175°C (350°F / Gas mark 4). Place 18 paper baking cases into muffin tins. Combine all the cupcake ingredients in a medium bowl and beat with an electric whisk until smooth and pale, about 2 to 3 minutes. Spoon the batter into the cases. Bake for 20 minutes. Remove the tins from the oven and cool for 5 minutes. Remove the cupcakes and cool on a rack.

To make the icing, gently heat the chocolate, coffee and butter in a small, heavy saucepan, stirring until melted. Remove from the heat and beat in the icing sugar. For each cupcake: Ice the top. Pipe or spoon marshmallow fluff on top of each cupcake. Double the pipe cleaner and insert both ends into the side of each cupcake wrapper to form a 'handle'.

Makes 1$^1/_2$ dozen

aquarium

see variations page 280

You don't have to leave home to visit the aquarium!

for the cupcakes
225 g (8 oz) unsalted butter, softened
115 g (4 oz) caster sugar
225 g (8 oz) self-raising flour
2 tsp baking powder
1 tsp salt
4 eggs
115 ml (4 fl oz) buttermilk
1½ tsp vanilla essence

for the icing & decorations
1 recipe Designer Buttercream (page 251)
blue food colouring
60 assorted gummy sea creature shapes
crushed nut biscuits

Preheat the oven to 175°C (350°F / Gas mark 4). Place 18 paper baking cases in muffin tins. Place all the ingredients in a medium bowl and beat with an electric whisk until smooth and pale, about 2 to 3 minutes. Spoon the mixture into the cases. Bake for 20 minutes or until a skewer inserted in the centre comes out clean.

Remove the tins from the oven and cool for 5 minutes. Remove the cupcakes and cool on a rack.

When the cupcakes have cooled, tint the buttercream sea blue. For each cupcake: Ice the top. Use a knife to make 'waves' on the top third of the cupcake. Place fish sweets and sea creatures among the waves. Scatter nut biscuits on the lower third of the cupcake to form the aquarium bed.

Makes 1½ dozen

garden hat

see variations page 281

Yellow cake, coloured icing, fruit-striped gum as bonnet trim, sugar pearls or flower sweets. Stacked vanilla wafers, iced over, form the peak of the hat.

for the cupcakes
225 g (8 oz) unsalted butter, softened
115 g (4 oz) caster sugar
225 g (8 oz) self-raising flour
2 tsp baking powder
1 tsp salt
4 eggs
115 ml (4 fl oz) buttermilk
1½ tsp vanilla essence

for the icing & decorations
1 recipe Designer Buttercream (page 251)
yellow food colouring
36 vanilla wafers
9 strips fruit-flavoured, striped sweets
coloured balls and flowers

Preheat the oven to 175°C (350°F / Gas mark 4). Place 18 paper baking cases in muffin tins. Place all the ingredients in a medium bowl and beat with an electric whisk until smooth and pale, about 2 to 3 minutes. Spoon the mixture into the cases. Bake for 20 minutes or until a skewer inserted in the centre comes out clean.

Remove the tins from the oven and cool for 5 minutes. Remove the cupcakes and cool on a rack. When the cupcakes have cooled, tint the buttercream yellow. For each cupcake: Ice the top. Sandwich two vanilla wafers together with buttercream and place in the centre of the cupcake. Ice over that. Cut one of the sweet strips in half lengthwise and form a band around the stacked wafers, notching the end. Decorate around the hat band with coloured balls and flowers.

Makes 1½ dozen

variations

day at the beach

see base recipe page 252

day on the lake
Prepare the basic cupcake recipe. Omit beach parasols and biscuit crumbs.
Tint all icing blue. For each cupcake: Ice the top, creating waves with a knife.
Place 3 small fish sweets among the waves. Thread a 5-cm (2-in) piece of
fruit stripe sweet through a coloured toothpick to make a sail, and insert
toothpick in centre of a thick orange fruit slice sweet. Place 'sailboat' in
centre of each cupcake.

day on the ski slope
Prepare the basic cupcake recipe. Omit beach parasols and biscuit crumbs.
Keep icing white. For each cupcake: Ice the top, mounding icing up on one
side to create a ski slope and dust with crystal sanding sugar. Tint Mouldable
White Chocolate dark green, divide it into 18 pieces, and cut each piece into
6 portions. Mould each portion into a 2½-cm (1-in) cone and snip randomly
and diagonally around the cone with kitchen shears. Gently lift out snipped
areas to form evergreen branches. Place 3 evergreen trees flanking each side
of the ski slope. Place a tiny plastic skier on the slope.

daisy daze

see base recipe page 255

black-eyed susan

Prepare the basic cupcake recipe. Substitute a combination of yellow and orange decorating sugars for yellow. Substitute plain chocolate chips for lemon sweets. For each cupcake: Ice the top. Place three plain chocolate chips in the centre. Snip each miniature marshmallow in half on the diagonal, dip on cut side in yellow–orange sugar and arrange sugared-side up around the centre like rows of petals.

dahlia

Prepare the basic cupcake recipe. Substitute a combination of red and orange decorating sugars for yellow. Substitute orange gumdrops for lemon sweets. For each cupcake: Ice the top. Place an orange gumdrop in the centre. Snip each miniature marshmallow in half on the diagonal, dip cut side in a mixture of orange and red sugar and arrange sugared-side up around the gumdrop like rows of petals.

zinnia

Prepare the basic cupcake recipe. Substitute a combination of red and pink decorating sugars for yellow. Substitute yellow gumdrops for lemon sweets. For each cupcake: Ice the top. Place a yellow gumdrop in the centre. Snip each miniature marshmallow in half on the diagonal, dip on cut side in a mixture of pink and red sugar and arrange sugared-side up around the gumdrop like rows of petals.

variations

clown

see base recipe page 257

princess

Prepare the basic cupcake recipe. Tint the melted white chocolate light pink, brush on the cones, and roll in pink and white sprinkles. Tint Mouldable White Chocolate pink, divide it into 18 pieces. Pinch off a small portion from each piece and roll into a ball. Roll the rest of the piece into a 40-cm (16-in) rope. Place the sugar cone firmly in the centre of each cupcake and secure the pink ball on the pointed end. Loop the rope around the circumference of the cone to make a ruffled edge. Scatter more sprinkles on the icing.

christmas tree

Prepare the basic cupcake recipe. Tint the melted white chocolate green, brush on the cones and roll in coloured sprinkles. Tint Mouldable White Chocolate yellow, divide it into 18 pieces. Pinch off a small portion from each piece and form it into a star. Roll the rest of the piece into a 40-cm (16-in) rope. Place the sugar cone firmly in the centre of each cupcake and secure the star on the pointed end. Loop the rope around the circumference of the cone to make a tree skirt. Scatter more coloured sprinkles on the icing.

variations

spider's web

see base recipe page 259

football
Prepare the basic cupcake recipe. For each cupcake, ice the top. Using a black gel icing tube, draw a hexagon in the centre of the cupcake. Draw a line from the point of the hexagon out to the edge of the cupcake. Omit gumdrops and pipe cleaners.

campfire
Prepare the basic cupcake recipe. Tint the buttercream green. For each cupcake, ice the top, but omit basic decorations. Cut thin chocolate-covered tube-shaped cookies or chocolates into 5-cm (2-in) 'logs' and stack in the centre of the cupcake. Cut strips of orange or yellow fruit-flavoured, striped sweets into 'flames' and place amidst the logs.

pot o' gold
Prepare the basic cupcake recipe. Tint the buttercream green. For each cupcake, ice the top, but omit basic decorations. Place a hollow chocolate cup in the centre of the cupcake. Fill with small gold-covered chocolate coins or gold nugget sweets. Arch a piece of rainbow licorice or rope sweets from one side of the cupcake to the other.

variations

how does your garden grow?

see base recipe page 260

strawberry fields forever
Prepare the basic cupcake recipe. Substitute small red sweets or balls for vegetable sweets.

magic bean garden
Prepare the basic cupcake recipe. Substitute small pastel jelly beans for vegetable sweets.

diggin' in the dirt
Prepare the basic cupcake recipe. Omit the coconut and vegetable sweets. Poke and enlarge 3 holes in the top of each cupcake and partially insert a gummy worm in each hole.

variations

bride doll

see base recipe page 262

princess doll
Prepare the basic cupcake recipe. Tint the buttercream a pale pink and use pink and purple sugar pearls and flowers.

bridesmaid doll
Prepare the basic cupcake recipe. Tint the buttercream a pale blue and use blue sugar pearls and flowers.

red carpet doll
Prepare the basic cupcake recipe. Tint the buttercream a dark blue or purple, smooth it over the body and sprinkle it with edible metallic glitter.

variations

ruffles & pearls

see base recipe page 265

raspberry ruffles & pearls
Prepare the basic cupcake recipe. Tint the buttercream and mouldable chocolate pale pink and flavour with raspberry flavouring. Sprinkle with pink sugar pearls.

lemon ruffles & pearls
Prepare the basic cupcake recipe. Tint the buttercream and mouldable chocolate pale yellow and flavour with lemon essence. Sprinkle with yellow sugar pearls.

mocha ruffles
Prepare the basic cupcake recipe. Instead of preparing Mouldable White Chocolate, substitute plain chocolate for the white chocolate and add 115 ml (4 fl oz) additional light golden syrup. Flavour the chocolate with 2 teaspoons coffee essence. Dust ruffles with cinnamon sugar.

morning latte

see base recipe page 266

hot chocolate
Prepare the basic cupcake recipe. Omit the coffee flavouring in the icing. Sprinkle chocolate sprinkles on top of each cupcake.

caramel macchiato
Prepare the basic cupcake recipe. Substitute prepared caramel ice cream syrup for the coffee flavouring in the icing. Drizzle prepared caramel ice cream syrup on top of each cupcake.

chai
Substitute 1½ recipes Chai Cupcakes (page 58) for basic Morning Latte cupcakes. Dust top of each cupcake with a mixture of 1 tablespoon raw sugar combined with 1 teaspoon each: ground cardamom, nutmeg, cloves and cinnamon.

variations

aquarium

see base recipe page 268

sea volcano

Tint half the buttercream sea blue, the other half orange–red. Omit the fish sweets. For each cupcake: Ice the top with blue. Use a knife to make 'waves' around the perimeter of the cupcake. Carefully trim the pointed end off a waffle sugar ice cream cone and place in the centre of the cupcake to make a volcano. Spoon or pipe orange–red icing to look like lava coming out of the volcano and down its side, to the sea below. Sprinkle the 'lava' with crushed nut biscuits.

gold miner's dream

Tint the buttercream sea blue. Omit the fish sweets. For each cupcake: Ice the top thickly with blue. Use a knife to make a 3-cm- (1½-in-) wide, meandering stream channel down the middle of the cupcake. Spoon yellow or gold decorating sugar and crushed nut biscuits in the channel.

bridge over troubled waters

Tint the buttercream sea blue. Omit the fish sweets. For each cupcake: Ice the top thickly with blue. Use a knife to make 'waves' around the perimeter of the cupcake. Lay a fruit-flavoured, striped sweet across the centre of the cupcake. Curve a pipe cleaner or chenille stick in a coordinating colour to arch over on either side of the sweet to form a suspension bridge.

variations

garden hat

see base recipe page 270

sombrero
Prepare the basic cupcake recipe. Omit the decorations. For each cupcake, ice the top. Place a large yellow gumdrop in the centre. Arrange miniature or small pieces of gumdrops in assorted colours around perimeter of the cupcake.

santa hat
Prepare the basic cupcake recipe. Omit the decorations. Leave half the buttercream white, the other half red. For each cupcake, ice the top with white. Carefully trim the pointed end off a waffle sugar ice cream cone and place the cone in the centre of the cupcake to make a Santa hat. Pipe red buttercream to cover the cone. Top with a large marshmallow.

red hat
Prepare the basic cupcake recipe. Tint the buttercream red. For each cupcake, ice the top. Sandwich two vanilla wafers together with buttercream and place in the centre of the cupcake. Ice over that. Press a 18-cm (7-in) stick of twisted black licorice to form a band around the stacked wafers, crossing the ends. Decorate around the hat band with red balls and flowers.

index

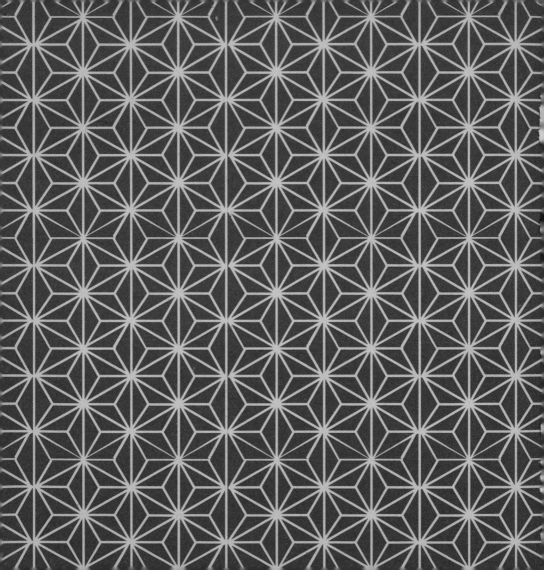